Praise for

DANGLING WITHOUT A ROPE
A Life Discovered

"Having grown up with the constrictive expectations of the 50's and 60's, fearless Bobbe Belmont, when presented with the option of adventure, was gone in a heartbeat into the exhilarating challenge of the limitless unknown. In Dangling Without a Rope, the reader is transported to volcanoes, glaciers, seas, jungles, rivers, and mountainsides all around the world as the grand, wild beauty of nature, with all its mystery and danger, offers a path for the never-say-never Bobbe to follow. Sometimes she wanders perilously off the trail, usually in a monsoon or a white-out, but with her indomitable spirit she never quits seeking the way."
~ Chet Ananda, author of *Memoir & Peace*

"Don't pick this book up unless you're ready to settle in with a cracking good read, because you won't be able to put it down, and when it ends, you'll want more. What sets Bobbe Belmont's story apart from other adventure narratives is that she's honest about her mistakes, and she learns as she goes. Here's a woman who played hard and paid for it, a woman who when faced by the greatest of all challenges, the loneliness and grinding daily fatigue of a debilitating chronic illness, rose above it by living well and mindfully, fearless in her determination to continue to love this world and each day in it."
~ Susan J. Tweit, author of *Walking Nature Home, A Life's Journey*

"Put yourself in Belmont's place in any of these stories and you'll be enthralled, terrified, glad to get out alive. Ask yourself, as she increasingly did, how and why she went headlong into such peril. Women, take a close look at her confessions of constantly bad choices in men. Men, shudder that you could have been one of her demons, then ask how you could have partnered with this tough, beautiful, ready-for-anything woman. Last and most important, read of her discovery of a new self, radiant in life beyond adventure, as failing health drags her within view of death's ugly den."

~ Alexander Drummond, author of *Enos Mills: Citizen of Nature*

"Barbara Belmont tells the exciting story of her adventures in remote and dangerous places from the Alps and Himalayas to the American Rockies and towering volcanoes in Bali. True grit and courage are the hallmarks of her journeys in some of the wildest places on the planet. A real page-turner."

~ John Lankford, author of *All the World is Wild and Strange, Stories Ironic and Ambiguous*

"I am convinced that Bobbe is the offspring of a whirling dervish and an over-eager bumper car. If you find yourself in her vicinity, stand back: The closer you are, the more likely you'll find yourself involved in an adventure of enormous danger and wild excitement. But read the book and find out for yourself. "

~ John Madsen, author of *Something Taken*

"What an inspiring book, Barbara Belmont! Anyone who doubts the possibilities of life should invest in this memoir. Most of us live content within the tight family, social, and geographical boundaries we were born to. Not Barbara, whose life is an ode to soulful adventures. The book narrates the story of a girl who flees her known world to explore unknown universes. Her determination never to give up is a journey in itself. Dangling Without a Rope is a vibrant book about a girl discovering the woman she never dreamed she would become."

~ Guy Tower, author of *A Middle East American*

"There is great hope and inspiration for anyone in Bobbe's book. Reading Dangling Without a Rope and watching Bobbe rock climb showcase her champion attributes: determination; the will to carry on and stay positive despite the circumstances; the ability to laugh at the odds and move forward. "

~ Robyn Erbesfield-Raboutou, author of *Sport Climbing with Robyn Erbesfield* and Four-Time World Cup Climbing Champion

"A story of the heartbreaking courage of one woman's extra-ordinary life, an amazing adventure and spiritual journey, strong and evocative."

~ Billy Hayes, author of *Midnight Express*

DANGLING
WITHOUT A ROPE

A Life Discovered

for 3/7/2021

Happy Birthday, Kez! You
being the scuba diving, roller-derbying
adventurous type, I thought you'd
really like this book written by a
woman I went to high school with.
Enjoy the read!

Love,
Jerry

Also by Barbara Belmont:

(and Richard Compton) *HIGHWHEELING: A Mountainbiker's Guide to Aspen and Snowmass,* Aspen, CO, (1986)

Photographer for *All the World is Wild and Strange, Stories Ironic and Ambiguous,* John E. Lankford, James A. Rock & Co., Florence, SC (2011)

DANGLING
WITHOUT A ROPE

A Life Discovered

Barbara Belmont

Foreword by Billy Hayes
Midnight Express

Front cover photography: *Bobbe in Boulder Canyon, 2011,*
by Bob Rubino, Blue Sky Photography.

Excerpt from 'Millennium', by David Whyte, in *Fire in the Earth,*
Poems by David Whyte © Many Rivers Press, Langley, WA.
Printed with permission from Many Rivers Press,
www.davidwhyte.com

ISBN: 1478286210
ISBN-13: 978-1478286219
Although this work depicts actual events, some names have been
changed to respect personal privacy.

Dedication

To the men of my adventures who died too young:
Andy Cox, Chuck Loukes, Rocky Keller, Neils Andersen
Johnny, Billy, and Guy Waterman.
Without you, I would not have become whom I was meant to be.

Contents

Foreword

Barbara was my beautiful high school friend, sometimes lover and kindred spirit, who became my eyes to the world through her letters and her adventures during my five years in Turkish prison. She was a brilliant, sophisticated woman who left the East, cut her long crimson fingernails down to working length, and gave up cities and society in favor of forests, mountains, and open skies. She rejected the values of her upbringing and the need to satisfy any standards but those she set for herself. She raced dog sleds in Alaska, climbed mountains in Nepal, traveled the globe, searching for an essence to life.

She was my touch of the feminine in the harsh masculine world of prison. I followed in her letters as she pedaled across the continent and wrote her poems of love from a dark prison cell...

> *Barbara bicycle somewhere in Europe,*
> *pump the strong steady measure of your legs,*
> *heartbreathing the land, a rolling world*
> *beneath rolling wheels...*
> *I would be a red streamer tassel swirling*
> *and dancing your wind...*
> *I would be a baseball card clothespin to the spokes*
> *— a low humming*
> *in your mind as you moved through the morning...*
> *I would be your hard leather seat...*

I hope the stories in this book lift, inspire and amaze its readers, just as they did me back when I so needed to be inspired and amazed by the heartbreaking courage of one woman's extraordinary life...

Billy Hayes
Midnight Express

Prologue

People who have heard my stories find them hard to believe. Let me assure you that each one truly happened in its own, remarkable way. Just how I managed to conceive of such adventures, step into the unknown, travel the globe, and stay alive is often a mystery to me. From a childhood prison of Catholic education and intense overprotection — the prison guards being my disturbed mother and a father who suffered endlessly from the trauma of World War II — I walked away and into a world of thrilling challenges and excitement.

While my peers were raising families and securing successful careers, I spent decades of my life single, curious about the planet, and totally mobile. One year I lived in 17 different dwellings. I also lived in vans, campers, trucks, cars, tents, yurts, huts, caves, and the out-of-doors. Often, the sum total of my belongings could fit in a VW Bug, sometimes a backpack. For every story that you read here, there are 10 more waiting to be told.

Between adventures I worked an absurd variety of jobs — chamber maid, salesgirl, *au pair*, gardener, grape and apple picker, ski teacher, coach, translator, florist, massage therapist, real estate agent, sled-dog racing consultant, kennel hand, secretary, switchboard operator, legislative assistant. When not earning a meager wage so that I could travel third class around the planet, I engaged in extreme sports. I climbed rock, mountains, and ice. I raced sled dogs, kayaked rivers and oceans, cycled alpine passes, piloted a hang-glider, flew an airplane, surfed, scuba dove... I competed every chance I got. I lived in a world of men. Women were simply not yet on the scene.

I undertook the writing of this book after hearing for 40 years: "You have *got* to write a book." Enough already! My adventures were dangerous. Luck was my constant companion — along with a good dose of naiveté. This is my telling of those tales. I have tried to confirm information where possible but acknowledge that the flavor and details of the events come from the deep, vibrant reservoir of my mind. The names of many of the people I encountered have been changed to protect their anonymity as have certain locations and dates.

I hope my stories will speak for themselves, make it all clear and unravel the mystery of how a timid, sheltered girl from New York became a wild, crazy woman of the world.

Barbara Belmont
September 2012
Jacksonville, FL

Chapter 1

ICE AXE

The Tetons, 1970

"That which does not kill us makes us stronger. ...When you look into an abyss, the abyss also looks into you."
~ *Friedrich Nietzsche*

I looked down the 1,000-foot, vertical snow wall I was about to descend on my own without a rope. A gaping crevasse where the glacier had separated from the rock of the mountain lay in wait 100 feet directly below me.

Traverse far left before dropping down, my silent voice commanded.

It was late in the morning. The sky was a cobalt blue, the mountains a pure, dazzling white. The air smelled of the freshness of melting snow, a perfect spring day. But it was too hot for a safe down climb; the snow was mush, like a slush cone. To be secure, I should have left three hours earlier.

I stood on the lip of the saddle between the majestic Grand Teton and its lesser sister, the Middle Teton. The brilliance of the snow blinded me. The 50-degree slope was so steep that I couldn't view the rift below me, but I'd seen the terrifying chasm three days earlier during

1

the ascent. Our climbing tracks had vanished; they'd melted out in the alpine sunshine. I planned to use them as a stairway down the icy wall. Without them I would have to kick a platform for each step all the way to the bottom. I was a rotten ice climber. I should not have been there.

Damn.

At the bottom of the snow bowl, I could see the spot I hoped to reach safely, outlined with boulders and cluttered with large snowballs that had rolled down the slope during the hottest part of the day and frozen in the night.

Silence pervaded the mountain sanctuary as I slammed the serrated pick of my ice axe into the headwall and stepped over the edge. I was alone in every sense of the word.

Some people are saved by religion. Me? Rock climbing. It was uncanny: I never thought of climbing, never yearned to climb, never knew a climber. I didn't think of myself as an athlete; no one else ever had. Ballet was my only early exercise: It proved a good foundation for the balance, coordination, and concentration climbing required.

I grew up itching to get away from the monotony of suburbia, the lines of traffic that stretched across Long Island, the boredom of a society that seemed single-mindedly focused on shopping and status. My discomfort went so deep that hidden clinical anxiety plagued my youth. Although I knew no other life, I felt imprisoned, hemmed in by Monopoly rows of tract houses with postage stamp green lawns. The lifestyle seemed unnatural, frenetic, mean, and ugly; the people were abrasive. I *had* to escape.

One glorious autumn day in 1968 at the age of 21, a friend of a friend invited me to go rock climbing with him. I said yes. I found myself standing on a carriage road in New Paltz, New York, in the midst of the world-famous rock climbing area, the Shawangunks (known to climbers as the "Gunks"). I tackled beginner climbs, sweating, trembling, terrified of falling. But the reward on the top overpowered all fear. The world lay below me. Hawks drifted on cliff currents at eye level. I felt I was conquering all that constrained my life. I was born on those crags.

I moved to New Paltz and became a climber. Once I discovered that life could actually offer emotional survival and self-discovery, I figured that moving even farther away from Long Island would facilitate my rescue. I looked for a way to do just that.

At the cliffs I met and charmed Ted. Theodore Gurney Brushmore IV, a trust funder, was getting a PhD in clinical psychology at Harvard. He was an intellectual snob, a political radical and an exuberant, though cautious, rock climber. Before long I was living in Cambridge, MA, as his girlfriend. There was no fire between us, but he offered me access to the richness of Cambridge life and a climbing partnership as well. He led; I followed. I liked it that way — everything to learn, nothing to lose.

We climbed with his friends, bright young men from Harvard and Yale. Weekdays we scaled the buildings in Harvard Yard or drove out to Quincy Quarries. After dark we often enjoyed little climbing/drinking parties in the apartment, practicing techniques like chimneying — backs halfway up the wall on one side of the hallway, feet on the other, spanning its width with our legs, maneuvering down its length. Weekends brought a mass exodus to the Gunks.

Excitement reigned as we planned our first climbing trip out West. Many of the people I knew from the Gunks would converge on the Tetons after the school year ended; we would be among them. The West held such allure: dramatic alpine peaks, famous routes on rock and snow, fierce animals, raging rivers. By the time Ted and I stuffed his racy, new BMW with our climbing and camping gear, I was obsessed with leaving the East. The thought of separating myself by thousands of miles from a miserable childhood and damaged parents swept me toward the Continental Divide.

The BMW's motor purred as the Heartland of America flew by. Speed became instantly addictive; I fought for my turn to drive. With the "Beemer" above 100 mph, I wondered which would explode first—the car from the velocity or me from the adrenaline rush. As we raced across the plains, the Rolling Stones blasted: "You can't always get what you want."

Yes I can.

And then the Rocky Mountains came into view—at first just a thin white line drawn across the mauve prairie, but soon a dramatic range stretching from north to south, the first real mountains to ever grace my vision. We headed northwest from Denver into a world of such drama and breadth, I could hardly believe it was real. The peaks contrasted sharply with the flat terrain of my past. The dry coolness of the high-altitude air replaced the cloying humidity of the East. Wildflowers splashed brilliant hues across the mountainsides.

Our climbers' camp clique consisted of Rocky, a Yale mathematician who worked at a sporting-goods store; Jackson, a stuffy Harvard law student; Ted, my psychologist boyfriend; and me. I was giddy with excitement from morning to night. For that summer we were "climbing bums," and although we could have passed for hippies with our holey jeans and scraggly hair, we were strong and driven athletes.

I never had girlfriends, not even as a child. Now I lived in a world populated by men. I related well to men. They made sense to me. Their practicality, team spirit, and daring appealed to me.

If there was another woman climber there that summer, I certainly do not remember her. It was me and the boys.

Under the tutelage of those companions, I developed quite a raunchy vocabulary. Cursing proved cathartic. My favorite expletive, learned from Ted, was "motherfucking, cocksucking, son of a bitch." I used it every chance I got—if my shoelace came undone or if I cracked a fingernail.

What would the nuns think of that? Ha!

We drank a good deal of beer around the campfire at night, Coors Beer. Coors was the beer of the West made from the water of pure mountain streams—or so the advertisements said. We couldn't buy it in the East back then, but we stocked up big time once we hit Wyoming. I discovered that I could drink the guys under the picnic table and proceeded to do so every night. That was the beginning of decades of hard drinking that went along with the climbing/adventuring life. Since neither of my parents drank, it was uncanny that I would become such a souse, that my tolerance for alcohol was so off the charts.

Exotic drugs like LSD and psychedelic mushrooms showed up in camp as well. One day I saw a rock-climbing flower child trip through knee-high meadows of purple lupine, screaming: "It's soooooooo beautiful, it's soooooooo fucking beautiful." Marijuana was abundant. I passed on the drugs. The Tetons transformed me. There was so much breaking loose to do to make up for the straightjacket world of my childhood. I was off to an excellent start.

Our domed mountaineering tents—cherry red, lemon yellow, and ginger orange—were strewn across the campsite like candies spilled from a box of Dots. Rocky, Ted, Jack, and I sat at a sticky picnic table, tempering our hangovers with black, instant coffee. A Whiskey Jack in brilliant blue and black plumage squawked its opinion from a branch above. Chipmunks flitted across the pine needle floor. The day had come to plan our ascent of the Grand Teton.

As far as I was concerned, the Grand was the ultimate mountain — 13,770 feet of awe-inspiring granite. It towered above the lesser peaks in the range, renowned for having the most compelling profile of any mountain in North America. At that point in my life I had never loved a person as much as I loved that mountain.

We decided to climb as two parties of two and chose the classic route, the Owen-Spalding, a highly exposed but technically easy climb. After all, that ascent would be the first alpine climb for all of us. We discussed what our packs would contain: food, water, clothing, rain gear, personal items, sleeping bags and pads, tents, climbing gear. I offered to bring along a couple of band aids in case we sliced up our fingers on the sharp granite.

A high-pressure front moved in overnight; the weather looked excellent for several days. We were acclimatized: The climb was on!

The brown Forest Service sign read: "Lupine Meadows Trailhead — 6,732 feet above sea level." The sign prepared me for the distance I would ascend, but not for the journey I was about to take.

A crisp, crystal-clear morning greeted us as we shouldered our packs and started up the trail. Base camp was on the lower saddle at 11,640 feet. We had more than five miles of hiking with 6,000 feet of elevation gain. It would take all day to get there. I needed help to heft my backpack onto my shoulders. I didn't wonder how I would carry it all that way but rather marveled that I was there carrying it at all.

The ascent was grueling. We were all sweating profusely within minutes, minutes that turned into hours in a timeless rhythm: step, relax, breathe; step, relax, breathe. I worked so hard my heart pounded in my skull. I tried to subdue my gasps, wanting the guys to think I wasn't fighting for every breath, that I was stronger than them. Mica sparkled on rock outcroppings along the steep trail. Ribbons of the Snake River glowed in the intense sunlight thousands of feet below. My shoulders and hips screamed pain. New, rigid mountaineering boots rapidly blistered my heels and ripped the skin, oozing and bleeding, to the bone. By the time we arrived at tree line, I could no longer feel the agony; my body's endorphins blocked it. Those endorphin highs would become another one of my addictions.

What I did feel was awe. I was now in a world of rock, snow, ice, and sky. Ephemeral waterfalls streaked the cliff walls. Granite spires rose around me. The mountain became my cathedral.

Record snows fell in 1970. The snow pack, which should have long since melted, covered our route between tree line and the lower saddle where we would pitch our tents. We expected to hike over moraine and through boulder fields to the headwall, climbing it with the aid of braided ropes affixed to the cliffs. Instead we encountered a massive basin filled with snow — not a rock or rope in sight.

A huge bergschrund, a cleft where the glacial ice separated from the rock of the mountain, lay ominously above us. The long, turquoise gash in the snow tapered from left, where it was wide enough to fit a freight train, to right, where it closed its deadly mouth. To reach the lower saddle, we would have to kick steps diagonally up and across the cirque and make sure we didn't slip and slide into the gaping crevasse. I gazed up and experienced a new emotion: terror.

We took out our ice axes; tied crampons to our boots. The going was gradual at first but became steeper and more treacherous as we got higher. I tried not to look up or down and definitely not *at* the monster bergschrund. One glance at the immensity of the precipitous landscape and I would have frozen like hardened steel. I focused on my boots, punching the spiky tips of the crampons into the ice one step at a time.

Why didn't we use a rope—especially once the crevasse lay below us? I have never been quite sure. It might have been that it was *de rigueur* to climb such snow slopes without a rope, or the guys were proving how fearless they were. I didn't voice my trepidation. I didn't want to be accused of being a weak woman who had no business on the mountain.

The step off the snow wall and onto the safety of the saddle was one of breathless relief. We arrived at our camp for the night, a moonscape of rock and boulders. Little islands of dirt covered in alpine vegetation made for excellent tent sites. We were close to 12,000 feet. The air was thin, chilly, brisk. We had the place to ourselves except for fat marmots that scurried from their perches atop big boulders and whistled dissatisfaction at our intrusion into their terrain.

The alarm jolted me awake at 4:30 a.m., and by first light we were underway. As the sun rose, the shadow of the Grand Teton stretched out across the flat plains of Idaho.

Where was I on that shadow outline?

We moved efficiently in two ropes of two, Rocky and Ted leading. The route was the easiest on the mountain. The rock was dry and grippy; I felt secure as I reached up for holds that awaited my hands. The air became thinner and cooler, yet my energy persisted. I was having the time of my life. The granite flashed; it was the finest rock I had ever climbed. I loved my body for its strength and my mind for its daring.

We summited late in the morning. No buffeting winds tried to rip our party off the peak. The indigo sky smiled down on a perfect climb. We celebrated with chocolate and water, hugs and kisses. The altitude intoxicated me. The morning's effort melted away as I reveled in a successful experience I had only dared to dream of. I stood atop a world with drop-dead gorgeous, 360-degree scenery below me. I felt privileged to reach the summit.

The descent required a long, free rappel with our two ropes tied together. Non-climbers often thought that rappelling was fun; actually it was quite dangerous. In those days, the rappel device, a piece of gear used as a brake on the rope, did not exist. Instead, you draped the rope over your shoulder and around your body, using its friction to slow you down. A failed anchor, entanglement in the rope, or slipping out of the rope would kill you. Usually climbers rapped down a wall by pushing gently away from the rock with their feet. Our route demanded a rappel into free air with a descent of 120 feet.

I pulled on my thick, leather gloves, checked to see that my pack was secure and that nothing might catch on the rope, and leaned out. It took an eternity to commit. My breath left me as I edged my boots down the wall. Suddenly, my feet flew out from under me, and I was on my way, dangling in space. I had never done a free rappel and had no idea of how tightly I needed to hold the rope. Of course, I held it too tightly at first and caused a dizzying, twirling spin. As I lowered myself, I hyperventilated; I wanted to throw up. I was certain I would plummet to my death. The only sound I heard was the hissing of rope over my mountain jacket as I lowered myself tentatively down my lifeline. And then—crunch! My boots hit the blessed rocks at the bottom.

"Good job, Barb," said Rocky, patting me on my back.

Yeah, right.

Soon we were back at camp. We had climbed the Grand Teton. What joy, what jubilation. We set an automatic timer and took a faux summit photo since we hadn't carried a camera with us to the top. I raised my ice axe above my head in victory, clearly a premature gesture.

Perfect weather greeted us the next morning. The guys slept late, then lounged around camp. I wanted to go early while the snow was set up from the below-freezing temperature of the night. And I wanted to be roped up. But the boys said that once the snow softened, it would be easier to kick steps. They thought that using a rope to belay the descent was for sissies.

I was becoming a lioness in many ways, but in the arena of confronting male authority, I remained a mouse. So while my male climbing partners lounged around enjoying the alpine morning, I worried but didn't speak up. Falling into the crevasse would mean death. I didn't want to die now when I was finally coming to life, but I had never been taught to weigh consequences, choose what was best for my well-being, or ask for what I needed.

I could think of only one solution: Leave before them. I could take my time, descend as conservatively as I wanted, stay safe. I packed my gear and left. Nobody cared. I hiked to the precipitous lip and mustered the courage to look down. Below, the steep terrain glistened menacingly. It was so far to the bottom.

I stepped over the lip.

I know I can do this. I have training. I... Focus!
The snow was too soft. I ever so cautiously kicked a step and moved my weight downward, aware that descending was more dangerous than ascending because gravity was pulling at me. The hot morning sun was like a hair dryer melting the icy slopes. I wondered if the bergschrund was still below me; the wall was far too steep to tell.

I took a step down. The snow collapsed beneath my foot; time stopped as the platform I stood on crumpled. Gravity grabbed me, and I started to fall. My top-heavy pack pulled me outward, head over heels. I did a somersault in the air and landed on my stomach facing uphill. That was the perfect position to dig in my ice axe and prevent a catastrophic slide. But my ice axe dragged through the snow like a knife through soft butter. I started ripping down the mountain.

I'm going to die.

I smelled the sweet, soft freshness of the snow as I flew downward. Ice tore at my face and clothes, abrading every exposed bit of flesh. A million tiny razor blades shredded my skin.

They will never find my body in the bergschrund.

But after careening down the slope for what seemed forever, I realized I was falling so rapidly that I flew right over the crack.

Still sliding, I looked up. A streak of bright red marked the line of my descent down the mountain. It didn't matter that I was bleeding profusely. I was alive.

Finally the slope relented. I was able to arrest the fall. Spread eagled on a still steep incline, I steadied myself and hacked a flat place into the ice so I could stand safely. As I unfastened my pack, three tiny figures gingerly began the descent from the saddle, moving with extreme caution. I could tell they saw me and the red stuff.

I choked on the bitter, iron taste of the blood. I dug into my pack and grabbed the top piece of clothing to use as a pad to staunch the flow, pressing hard. With my free hand, I grabbed fistfuls of snow and tried to wash the gore from my body.

The scene was surreal—a perfect mountain morning drenched in blood. I felt no emotion. My heart stopped pounding. I detached myself. Experiencing the horror would have been dangerously debilitating. I had to keep my wits, take care of myself.

Gotta stop the bleeding and figure out what's happened to my face.

I couldn't feel my upper teeth at all, so I figured I'd knocked them all out. I spit out mouthfuls of viscous crimson fluid, watching for any teeth I hadn't swallowed. The left side of my face was numb. Blood was drenching my clothes and saturating the platform. My vision blurred.

I considered the possibility of a facial wound. If the skin was ripped open, I could butterfly it with my three band aids. Just as I reached for the mirror, Rocky, the brave one, arrived. I had forgotten about my companions. He called out:

"Barb, what are you doing?"

"I'm looking for my mirror so I can see what happened to my face."

"You don't want to do that. Here, give me that mirror. I'll help you."

Ted came next, looked at me and heaved. Jackson arrived last. He paled and retreated to where Ted was standing with his back turned to me.

When I somersaulted, the serrated pick of the ice axe drove through my cheek, back to my brain, and up to my eye, fracturing the cheekbone and the orbital rim and floor. There was a gaping hole in my face the size of my fist. I felt nothing because I had severed all the nerves.

Rocky was the most cool-headed person I ever encountered.

"This isn't as bad as it seems. You've got a cut on your face, but you know how head injuries bleed like crazy. I'll get you fixed up in no time." His confidence flooded me with relief.

I was drifting off, watching the scene from outside myself. Calmness came. I hadn't fallen into the crevasse. I was alive. I was bleeding, but someone was helping me. Rocky's kind eyes, like quiet black pools, embraced me with what I interpreted as love as he carefully tried to clean me up with a dirty tee shirt from my pack. He made balls of the slushy, wet snow and washed my face, neck, arms with it. He smiled.

"Get the band aids out of my pack so we can butterfly the cut. I know how to do it," I said.

"I know how to do it, too," he said. "Just relax and let me take care of you."

Someone wants to take care of me.

He used the band aids to placate me. My face needed much more than band aids. He folded his filthy bandana into a compress and instructed me to keep pressure on my cheek while he conferred with the others. I watched them whispering as acrid blood dripped down the back of my throat. Everything was like a dream.

They decided that two of them should stay with me while the strongest downhill runner sprinted to the trailhead and called for a helicopter. I knew if I were taken off the mountain in a chopper, my name would end up in the accident report section of the American Alpine Journal. If I were ever written up in the Journal, I wanted it to be for a first ascent, not a Flight for Life rescue. I pulled myself back into my body and insisted on walking out.

The guys loaded my belongings into their packs and roped me up between them. My equilibrium was bad. It was a challenge not to trip, not to step off the edge, to stay conscious. My awareness came and went, but I put one foot in front of the other all the way to the parking lot. It took me four hours to get down. For the rest of my life, I'd know how to put one foot in front of the other no matter how hard the task at hand.

Twice a party of mountaineers heading up passed us. My only recollection was the expression of those men when they saw my blood-soaked body. I felt embarrassed messing up the pristine wilderness like that.

———

I was lying in Jackson Hole on a white sheet soiled with my dirt, sweat, and blood when an ER doc entered the room. He used the longest needle I ever saw to numb my wound and put his fingers into the cavity that had been the left side of my face. I watched his hand disappear into my head.

"You've really done some serious damage, young lady. You've fractured all the bones on the left side of your face. You're lucky as hell that your brain isn't damaged. I have no idea what is holding your eyeball in place. It should be in your mouth." Dr. Tact.

Pushing the BMW to impossible speeds, Ted drove me to Salt Lake City, the location of the nearest surgeon qualified to do the kind of intricate surgery I needed. The daily flight out of Jackson had already left, so driving was the next fastest way to go. By the end of the day I was checked into the hospital. Luck was with me in more ways than one. My plastic surgeon was one of the best in the country — *and* he was a mountaineer and the doctor on the first American Everest Expedition in 1963.

He explained that an infection had set in, and therefore he couldn't use plastic to reconstruct my face. He would make incisions under my eyelid, inside my nose, and inside my mouth from my nose to my jaw. Then he would find as many pieces of bone as he could and put them back in place. My face — his jigsaw puzzle. Finally he would pack the cheek internally with gauze to hold the fragments secure until the bones knitted together. Later a second incision would be made inside my mouth above my teeth; the gauze would be drawn out through that slit. Thank goodness I didn't know at the time that this final procedure would be done while I was awake and watching.

Ted sat in on the consult, then followed me down the hall to my hospital bed.

"There's no sense in my hanging around, can't do anything. Besides I don't want to miss any climbing. You're going to be here for quite a while. I'll call in a few weeks. Maybe I can pick you up and drive you back East at the end of my vacation."

This guy, this Harvard trust funder, psychologist — whom I definitely no longer considered my boyfriend — was unequipped to deal with my terrifying situation. Best to run, and run he did. I

14

watched in disbelief as he disappeared down the cold, sterile hallway. When I awoke from the seven-hour surgery, wrapped from the neck up like a mummy, I was alone.

But my wonderful doctor dropped in every day and sometimes in the middle of the night after an emergency surgery. He salved my suffering with tales of rock climbing in Utah, the conquest of Everest, skiing champagne powder. He promised that he would take me to Alta and teach me to ski the steep and deep the following winter. In the depths of agony, I fell in love with that handsome, compassionate man.

When the bandages were about to come off, he came into the room. He took my hand and explained that he did not know whether I had lost the sight in my left eye or whether I would have double vision permanently. He also explained that it could take a year for my face to heal and that I would experience significant pain in the interim.

During those many weeks in the hospital the oddest thing happened: I changed. Coming so close to death stirred a deeper consciousness of which I had not been aware. I heard the tiniest sounds. I smelled not just the hospital smells, but the perfume of visitors walking down the hall, the clean smell of my dear doctor as he sat on the edge of my bed, the sweet breeze that entered my window each morning. I became aware of the fine line between life and death and how I walked it every moment of my existence. I lost fear. I became euphoric. The joy of being alive — no matter what I looked like or whether I had my vision — filled my painful days. An invisible grin sat continually on my swollen, distorted face. The happiness of survival sang a song in the cells of my body.

I returned to Salt Lake City the following February and skied waist-deep powder with my charming doc. He took

pictures of my face for a professional presentation; I had healed miraculously well. He was proud; I was beautiful.

I went on to climb two other famous routes on the Grand the following year with intact vision and a full mouth of teeth. Today there are over 90 routes on the mountain.

The Grand Teton continues to inspire people from around the world as a first alpine ascent. Now two excellent guide services lead many of them to the top. The mountain crawls with climbers. Exum Guides maintain a hut on the lower saddle. They have a chemical toilet surrounded by a three-foot high rock wall. The view into Idaho from the crapper is reputed to be superb.

Chapter 2

HIGH SIERRA

California, 1971

"We are made to persist. That's how we find out who we are."
~ Tobias Wolff

Yosemite Valley—one of the most awe-inspiring places on earth. Tourists imagine this paradise bounded by the dramatic granite walls that define it.   But vertiginous trails lead vertically up and out of the valley into an enchanted wilderness of peaks and domes, the high country of Yosemite. It was there that I discovered the rigors and dangers of ski mountaineering and the indomitable spirit that allowed me to survive.

It was Spring, and I was on the lam like a prisoner who'd dug the perfect tunnel and escaped her lifetime penitentiary sentence. In the heartbeat when I realized that I loved to climb, travel, and adventure far more than I would ever love to work, get a graduate degree, or have a husband and babies, I became emancipated and graduated to the status of official climbing bum.

I met Michael climbing at the Gunks in the autumn of '68, and we became good friends. He was five years my junior, one year out of high school, and as eager as I was to travel west in his forest green Dodge hippie van. I was embarrassed to take off with a teenager, but Michael looked older than his age, so it wasn't too obvious that I was robbing the proverbial cradle.

He grew up in northern Minnesota, a blue-eyed Scotsman, tall and lean, with silky locks that hung over his stiff eyebrows. At the age of seven, his father sent him alone into the wilderness — a sort of northern walkabout. He'd adventured ever since.

The kid was bright, a vibrant combination of intellectual sophistication and primitive mountain man. Challenging intellectual discussions were a major part of our daily routine. He *did* like to have his way, to always be right. Since I didn't possess that personality trait, it wasn't hard to acquiesce when tensions rose. By the time we arrived in Yosemite Valley it was April, and a couple's dynamic was firmly in place. I knew how to play that role all too well; I'd done it with my father my entire childhood.

So there I was, thinking I was a free spirit while ceding all my power to an 18-year old.

———————————

Yosemite was a mind-boggling experience for me. I had seen many Ansel Adams photographs and read countless articles in climbing magazines about the beauty of the place, but nothing could prepare me for the real thing. The snows from the mountains had begun their seasonal melt, and the pellucid Merced River flowed swift and cold. Steely granite walls, thousands of feet high, were painted a darker shade of gray by gossamer waterfalls that sang as they drifted downward. The lush green floor of the valley teemed with wildflowers in a rainbow of hues.

We headed for Camp IV, the haunt of climbing legends like Royal Robbins and Yvon Chouinard. This campground was a man's place; rarely did I see another female. What a treat to be surrounded by so many shirtless, buff rock masters.

Climbing gear and clothes sat piled high on most camp tables. A slack line was strung between two solid evergreens. While empty beer bottles were strewn about, there were no coolers visible. Food was stored in vehicles because wild animals often came looking for a meal. We found an empty site and pitched our tent. This was our home for the next few months.

Our first night in camp was memorable. We had a few beers, then snuggled into our sleeping bags. I awoke in the middle of the night.

Why is Michael rolling over onto me?

But Michael was on my left, and the weight was on my right. I opened my eyes. Moonlight filtered into the tent; I could see that the flimsy nylon structure bowed inward. Something nudged the side of my head. I felt hot breath through the diaphanous fabric. My heart raced. There was a noise not unlike the oinking of a pig at my ear, loud and clear. Sniff, sniff, sniff. Push, push. Grunt, grunt, grunt.

Then I knew. Those were no pig sounds. They were ursine inhalations. A bear was leaning on me, smelling me. I wanted to run but couldn't move. I felt frozen, as if trapped in cement. I wanted Michael to wake up and protect me, but I was too frightened to speak. I poked him repeatedly to no avail.

"Michael, Michael, wake up," I finally whispered.

He moaned in his sleep. I tried again: "Michael, help."

"What..."

"Sh-h-h-h," I murmured. "A bear."

The tent swayed under the bear's weight. It was now that my brave boy surprised me: He heard the snorting and went still, powerless to deal with the situation. We lay immobilized, like two corpses on a slab, acceding to the bear's explorations until it sauntered off in search of a more lucrative location for junk food.

We were lucky.

I'd imagined my perfect outdoorsman as someone who could confront a bear and scare it away despite his fear. Even so, I still didn't doubt his leadership. I needed him to lead us, to see that we remained safe. I depended on his experience.

Michael's major goal for the spring season was to climb The Nose on El Capitan, one of the most famous great walls on the planet. Our friend, Johnny, from the Gunks, would join us in a few weeks to climb it with him. In those days El Cap was a multi-day aid climb—not my cup of tea. I did not hanker to spend days on a 3,000 foot wall, banging in pitons, attaching slings to use as ladders for ascension. I'd heard how painfully laborious it was hauling up all the gear, food, and water, pitch after pitch, day after day. Nor was I fond of the idea of sleeping on a platform suspended from pitons with nothing but thousands of feet of crystalline air beneath me. No, the guys could have El Cap. I wanted to climb lesser routes and be "home" at night to drink a beer and ogle all my gorgeous climbing idols. I decided that when Johnny and Michael did climb El Cap, I would hike up the descent trail with brownies and hot chocolate to greet them at the top.

Michael had an expedition mentality and soon grew bored free climbing easier routes with me. Climbs needed to be long and hard to satisfy him. That was why after a week of rock climbing, he hatched the idea to initiate me into the world of high altitude, back-country ski mountaineering and planned an expedition worthy of his ambitious nature.

"Barb. I've got an awesome idea. Let's go find some ski mountaineering equipment and take a week-long tour in the high country."

"Cool, Michael. Fantastic idea. But you know I've never skied."

"No problem. I can teach you when we hit snow country. You'll be a natural. You'll *love* it."

Michael was hardened early by multi-day ski tours with his dad in the frigid northern woods. His sense of easy would be anyone else's idea of extreme, outrageous or impossible, but I was far too artless to realize the risks inherent in his plans.

We left the moist, tranquil beauty of the Valley and headed into arid Modesto, the location of the nearest Army Navy Surplus Store. Michael knew exactly what we needed in lieu of lightweight, efficient, comfortable gear, which we couldn't afford.

"Good day, sir," said my ever polite companion to the man behind the counter. "We're looking for two pairs of World War II skis and two pairs of bear trap bindings with leather straps."

"You kids are in luck. I have both. But what in the world do you want with those ancient things?"

"We're planning a little ski tour. They fit within our budget."

"The young lady here isn't going to be skiing on those monstrous planks, is she?"

"Yes she is, sir. She'll do just fine."

The laminated, 1941-vintage, hickory skis we purchased were similar to those used by the illustrious 10th Mountain Ski Division, but theirs had metal edges — ours did not. They weighed more than 18 pounds and were 7'6" long. I was 5'4". The 10th Mountain used bear trap bindings with a cable fitted around the heel of the ski boot for safety and convenience. We put our rigid mountaineering boots into the metal toe piece and strapped the boots straight to the skis. I later learned that this was called a "death trap" binding because, in the event of a fall, there was no possibility of release from the binding. Of course, Michael never fell.

"Gee, Barb, I'm thinkin' those skis could be a might heavy for you. Let's swing by Chouinard's shop and see if we can borrow his rip saw to make them a tad narrower."

I said: "Could you make them a *tad* shorter while you're at it?"

"Nope. Would ruin the dynamics of the ski. You'll just have to learn to live with the length."

As we reentered the Valley with my new, slimmer skis, I cogitated: *How can these skis be this narrow and still be stable enough to balance, much less glide on? And how am I going to learn to ski with a 60-pound pack on my back?*

I could barely carry a pack that heavy on solid ground.

The morning of our departure dawned a brilliant blue. Birds trilled and chipmunks zipped about the campground. I thought it a shame to leave the delights of spring for a world frozen in snow 50 feet deep, but Michael whistled some Scottish ditty his grandfather taught him and packed up a storm.

We split the communal gear equally. He said I needed to carry my weight and not be girlish, so my backpack bulged with the gear, clothing, and food I would require for a week of snow camping with subfreezing nights. Then he strapped the hickory sticks onto my pack. They stuck up above my head like the ears of some overgrown rabbit, while the tails hovered just three inches above the ground and snagged when I stepped down or over a rock. I consoled myself with the thought that once we hiked up out of the Valley and hit the snow line, I could put them on.

Contour maps indicated we would gain upwards of 5,000 feet in elevation. We would hike to snowline, then ski our way across the high country to the trans-Sierra Tioga Pass Road and down to a paved highway from where we would hitch back into the Valley. Michael controlled the planning, the map, the compass, the food, the fuel, the rest breaks. Me? I was the hapless novice.

Sunlight filtered through a translucent mist caused by the dramatic, voluminous waterfalls playing the music of sprites. A heavenly smell of fresh sap flowing in the warmth of the spring sun permeated the air. The steps of the trail rose relentlessly into a towering ponderosa forest. Sweat ran like small rivers between my breasts. My mountaineering boots were steel hard, and the steepness caused unsettling dynamics between leather and skin. Before the first hour was up, blisters filled with lymph and blood blossomed on my feet.

We both wore knickers with wool knee socks. What a sight we must have been, clawing our way upward under those heavy packs with outdated clothing and WWII skis.

All was still but for my heaving breaths and the pounding of the river below. No other hikers were headed our way. In fact, we expected to be alone the entire trip. The majestic walls of the Valley changed perspective but remained imposing as we gained altitude. The air cooled, hinting at the snow world above. The first chill was invigorating and a great relief. I struggled under the weight of my burden, but Michael permitted only a five-minute rest every hour. My pack straps dug into my shoulders and raised aching welts. Spells of dizziness came and went; sometimes I wanted to cry. Michael, the ultimate taskmaster, refused to slacken the pace.

We ascended through Jeffrey pines and white firs at a less steep pitch. Patches of snow began to appear under the shade of trees. Gargantuan pinecones littered the needled floor. We did not speak — Michael, because he treated the expedition as a religious experience; me, because I couldn't catch my breath.

We reached snowline as the stunning vistas shifted from the walls of the Valley to the domes and vertical cliff faces of the high country. A pristine wilderness stretched before us like an endless down comforter enclosed in a white velvet cover.

The climb out had been so strenuous that I wondered if I could possibly strap on those skis the following morning and continue. My teenage boss had no remorse for the punishment he inflicted on me. It should have been obvious that the expedition we were undertaking required three things: extreme endurance, solid backcountry skills, and ski mountaineering expertise. I lacked all three and wondered if Michael wasn't a burgeoning misogynist in disguise.

Mercifully, at dusk, we camped. Michael did all the cooking and cleaning up. I couldn't complain, only collapse. The temperature plummeted below freezing, and I could not get warm in my new, 40 below zero, down sleeping bag. In the morning, I crawled out, feeling like I had been hit by a Mack truck. Every muscle in my body screamed with pain. I had quarter-size holes in my heels, worn to the bone by my rigid boots. Michael whistled away as he prepared oatmeal and hot jello, sublime in his element.

He helped me strap on the skis and hefted my pack onto my shoulders. He showed me how to put my hands through the straps of the 40's vintage poles, which were bamboo with baskets the size of frisbees. Everything seemed awkward. Balancing was tenuous, so I relied heavily on the poles, fatiguing my upper body within minutes.

How will I ever manage days of this?

The moment of truth was upon me; I had to learn to ski right then and there. Michael had put gooey klister wax on the bottom of our skis to grip the snow and help us climb. I moved upward slowly, struggling for equilibrium, both physically and mentally. Instead of keeping them behind me, I dug my poles in at my sides to keep from falling. As a result I slid backwards with every step. It seemed impossible to maneuver those awkward, heavy boards over the water-ice snow.

Michael taught me to herringbone uphill. "Walk like a duck. Stand on your inside edges. Keep your poles behind you."

Ducks quack. I'm the quack for being out here with you, Michael.

The entire experience was excruciating. Yet, I stayed in the moment, blacked out all the falls I had already taken and avoided thoughts of what was yet to come. As my energy slipped away, we encountered our first downhill terrain. It was gradual, but this was my first descent ever.

"Barb. Broaden you stance. Now put the tips together, bend your knees, and slowly descend, following my line."

I made a V of the skis, using the poles to keep me in place. When I released the poles, I started moving, the ski tips came apart, and I found myself ripping down the slope. I saw a run out at the bottom of the hill and hoped that the terrain would stop me. I barreled downward, fixed in a rigid position, arms spread wide, knees locked, aghast at my acceleration.

I shifted my weight onto my left ski. It dug deeply into the snow, drawing me more to my left side. I fell hard. My skis stuck out of the snow at odd angles. I was stranded on my back, held prisoner by my pack and struggled like a turtle stuck upside down in its shell. It took five, frustrating minutes to shed the pack, rearrange the skis, learn to stand perpendicular to the fall line, shake off all the snow, and start off. Five seconds later, I fell again.

While Michael set up our tent for the second evening, I sat on my pack and silently wept. This had been the most demanding day yet in my new adventure life. I had sprained, strained, battered, and bruised every square inch of my body. My blisters were becoming infected and hurt like hell. Michael's Scottish ditties were driving me crazy. I decided that I hated this boy and wondered how many months they would take to find his body if I killed him on the spot.

Yet I learned something invaluable that day. I learned to take one fall at a time, get up again and persevere in the face of what seemed impossible odds. I also discovered I was one tough chick.

The weather shifted that night. A vicious spring storm descended upon the only two people in the high country of the Sierra Nevada Mountains. The storm began as a distant hum, then calamity struck. Ice pellets hammered the tent walls: rat-a-tat-tat, rat-a-tat-tat. The hum turned to a roar.

I put on all my clothes and wrapped my sleeping bag around me, but couldn't get warm. I devoured my freeze-dried dinner and drank several cups of tea, yet shivered uncontrollably. The storm shut off the main switch to my internal furnace. Outside the conditions continued to deteriorate. I was grateful for our little shelter, yet it seemed so fragile against the forces of nature that conspired against us. If we had slept outdoors, the rapid accumulation of heavy snow would have buried us immediately. Instead it buried our shelter.

Blizzard gusts flattened the tent and forced us onto our bellies. I feared it would be ripped away with us in it, but Michael had secured it with long snow stakes, and it held firm. I hoped the wind would not shred it to pieces.

"Barb. I'm going to start shoveling every 15 minutes. Otherwise the snow will trap us inside." He dressed, grabbed the little avalanche shovel, and disappeared into the darkness. As he reentered from the storm plastered in "Sierra cement" he looked like a Yeti, his eyelids stuck together with rime ice. No Scottish ditties now. "Breathing out there is almost impossible. It's like inhaling a snow cone. I'll need to cover my face next time I go out."

Michael boiled more water, made hot chocolate for us both, and shut the stove down. I slugged down the hot, sweet liquid.

"Michael. I'm freezing. Could you please turn the stove back on and melt another pot of snow for tea?"

We were using a Primus, a white gas stove. Annoyed, Michael pumped it several times and struck a match. POP! An orange blaze exploded in the tent as the fumes from the stove caught fire in the confined space. Flames rose from my wool knicker socks, both sleeping bags ignited, and my long hair sizzled with an immediate, nauseating stench. The whole tent seemed ablaze. Panic flowed from my pores like lava from a volcano. We beat down the flames with our gloved hands until every spark was out.

We sat speechless and took in the damage — my socks, hair, pants, shirt, and parka were burned, as were our sleeping bags. The tent was scorched in several places, but Michael's wet clothing kept him from burning. The place stunk of fumes and singed hair. Our clothing would still provide us with protective cover in the morning.

"Barb, I think we'd better shorten our route and get out of here. Breaking trail will be really tough with the new snow. We need to get to the road as directly as possible and high tail it down to the highway."

Amen to that.

Michael was in and out of our ravaged shelter all night, scooping away the leaden snow before it could collapse the tent. Each time he came inside, we huddled together to try and stay warm. Sleep evaded us.

As dawn cast its purplish pink hue on a world of white, we extricated ourselves and gave thanks that the snow had stopped and the sky was clearing. Dampness permeated everything we wore and carried with us. I consoled myself with the thought that once we dug out our belongings, skiing in two feet of fresh, heavy snow would warm me rapidly.

We bee lined it to the Tioga Pass Road, crossing dangerous avalanche terrain and traversing a cirque with a 500 foot drop. I looked down the dizzying incline, took short gulps of air, and slid my skis cautiously in Michael's trail. My body trembled with the effort to remain balanced. Michael gave me no avalanche instruction, so if we were caught in an avalanche, the chance of my swimming out of it was nil. He labored in silence, making a deep, consistent track. He insisted we keep far apart on the steep traverse so that if one of us did set off an avalanche, the other would not also be drawn into it.

What will I do if I can't go on?

My stamina and nerves were fried. I knew one more day of trudging down the snow-covered road to civilization lay in front of us. The thought of another night in the tent with yet another day of skiing to follow was baneful to me.

"Barb, I think I see the road. Do you see the snow stakes peeking out? Let's head that way and see if we can pull off a few more hours before we camp."

The snow-laden tops of those stakes were like little angels hovering along the path. The dangerous cross-country skiing was over. The road was a thread that connected us to civilization. My body screamed pain and fatigue, but my spirit was eager to ski as far as possible that day.

The silence spoke volumes about the wilderness we traversed. No bird song, no jet hum, not the whisper of a breeze — just our labored sounds as we struggled under our loads on our heavy, long skis.

We had followed the road about an hour when I heard something mechanical and grating, not of nature. As we came around a curve, a sight presented itself that came as close to heaven as I could wish for: A huge snowplow was at work and pavement—beautiful, black, wet pavement—shone beyond it. Our rescue was at hand.

"What the hell?" said the driver as we jumped up and down and shouted over the noise of the snowplow to catch his attention. I inhaled the offensive fumes of the diesel and thought a bouquet of roses couldn't smell sweeter. "Where did you kids come from?"

We told him our story.

"It's just about quitting time," he said. "Get in, and I'll take you down the road to my car. I'd be pleased to drive you to your campsite, since you won't find any traffic for hitching up here."

Back in Yosemite, the climate between Michael and me was as cold as the valley was warm. We talked little until Johnny arrived a week later. When I contemplated the adventure we had undertaken and remembered the sound and the fury of the storm, I was seriously shaken. For all Michael's knowledge and skill, he made a near-lethal mistake when he put a novice into such a technically and physically demanding situation.

I learned to persist beyond my limits and was grateful to survive, but luck played a major role in getting out alive.

———

The high country of Yosemite is now a popular place to ski tour. Touring companies guide people, cabins give shelter, an upscale lodge provides creature comforts. The wilderness is tamer and safer. People traverse established, marked routes. They use GPS for directional guidance. They wear space age technology clothing.

My introduction to cross-country skiing should have soured me on the sport. So how do I explain this unlikely outcome: Cross-country skiing became the primary sport of my life for over a decade. I earned certification both as a teacher and coach in Switzerland. I taught the disabled. I ran a x-c ski school in California

and directed a ski school in Aspen. I raced internationally and skied into the field of the women's elite racers in the Engadine Ski Marathon. During those years, I spent seven days a week on skis—on snow in winter and spring, on glaciers in summer and fall. I became better at skiing than at walking. Perhaps I have Michael to thank.

Chapter 3

MUSHER

Alaska, 1972 / 1973

"The way is the goal."

~ *The Buddha*

Alaska. Land of superlatives. Consummate mountains, peerless northern lights, unsurpassed wildlife, supreme wilderness. I made a pilgrimage to Alaska with a mountain in my mind. Instead I found a stunning, freeing, new way of life.

The small, red, Willys Jeep bounced north over the Alcan Highway through oceans of dark green conifers. Moose, grizzly bears, and wolves surprised us on hidden corners of the undulating road. The four-seater, four-wheel drive jeep contained four large men, the climbing gear required to attempt a daring first-ascent on Mt. Huntington in the McKinley Range, and *moi*. It reminded me of the '60s fad of seeing how many bodies you could stuff into a telephone booth. I was crushed between the roof and mountains of gear, one arm extended toward the ceiling, trying to protect my head each time we pounded over a rut. Millions of potholes punctuated those endless miles. I felt certain we hit every one.

The 1,000 miles of dirt highway were like a dust-worm squirming its way toward the Alaskan border. My traveling companions—Neils, Rocky, Frank, and Johnny—were dear friends and accomplished mountaineers. We wore sweaty red bandanas over our faces to keep the dust out of our lungs, yet our eyes remained teary from the irritation, and everyone hacked with a dry cough. We drove round the clock despite the discomfort of the traveling arrangements, eager for an adventure of a caliber none of us had ever experienced. This would be an expedition to surpass any yet accomplished in North America.

What was my role in the climbing odyssey? Was I also ready to risk life and limb and dance with extreme avalanche danger? Hell, no. I talked my way into being the camp cook and maid. My past mountaineering disasters proved that I lacked the skills to climb the mountain. Yet my lowly role would afford me the opportunity to fly through the high-altitude paradise of the McKinley Range onto the Ruth Glacier and be present as the guys attempted their assault. Once they left base camp, I would live alone and hope that the constant avalanches for which the mountain was renowned wouldn't wipe the camp away with me in it. To be alone in a brilliant white amphitheater of rock and ice with the giants of that great massif watching over me called to my wildest instincts.

———————

By the time we reached Anchorage, the cough I blamed on the dust had worsened markedly. I stumbled into an antiseptic medical clinic set up for the Native American street people and waited my turn in a line of sickly, alcoholic folks. The lives of the Alaskan Indians depressed me as did my diagnosis: walking pneumonia. The doc prescribed antibiotics and gave me strict instructions for bed rest.

"I know some people in Willow, north of Wasilla. They have a big house and perhaps could put you up while we're away," suggested Rocky.

I knew my crew would be gone for many weeks if good weather welcomed them, even longer if they had to wait out spring storms. A dismal cloud hung over me, for I couldn't bear the thought of missing my thrill-of-a-lifetime, ultimate mountain experience.

Rocky got on the phone and made the call. He returned to the waiting room, a big grin on his face. We'd all been extended a hearty, Alaskan welcome. We headed for Willow.

A massive herd of elk grazed lazily on the left side of the highway as we departed Anchorage. Bald eagles drifted and swooped on air currents above tidal flats. The McKinley Range peeked out 20,000 feet above us, sparkling like a high-grade diamond necklace in the distance.

Willow was a tiny community with mostly ramshackle cabins hidden in the bush. A mining boom started when gold was found on Willow Creek in 1873. In 1920 the Alaska Railroad built a station with a small kitchen, a bar, a poolroom, and a post office. The locals still gravitated there for community; that structure was the heart of Willow. The population numbered 78 people, one last, untrapped lynx, many enormous moose, and an occasional, roving wolf.

We found Mile Marker 66 indicating our turn and drove on a short dirt road toward a surprisingly large, modern house. A horse barn and pond stood off to the left. All we could see from the parking lot was the back of the home. We stepped from the jeep with great curiosity.

"Ah-wohhhhh" was the sound of a single howl; I thought it had to be a wolf. The sound was unearthly, causing the hair on my arms to stand up with some primeval response. A second, lingering howl was added to the first, then hundreds more. This was the famous Howling Dog Farm. As we walked toward the front of the house, doghouses fanned out as far as the eye could see. 345 Siberian Huskies, Malamutes, Indian dogs, Eskimo dogs and mutts—each chained to its own house—greeted us with their canine "Ode to Joy," a siren song that sang in my heart from that day forward.

The story of Earl and Natalie Norris was a remarkable and romantic tale that belonged to the history of modern Alaska. After WW II, Earl left Idaho to settle in Anchorage and run sled dogs. Natalie, a young musher from Lake Placid, NY, decided to head for Alaska as well. Earl saw her picture on a magazine cover; the inside article talked about her interest in sled dogs and her dream of a life in the Far North. Earl was instantly smitten and wrote to offer to meet her at the train station.

They married and homesteaded in what eventually became downtown Anchorage. When they sold that dog farm for big bucks, they moved in comfort to Willow. Earl was at the heart of the renewal of sled dog racing in North America and initiated the World Sled Dog Racing Championships at the Anchorage Fur Rendezvous in 1946. The Norrises were aptly known as the "Pioneers of Modern Sled Dog Racing." Their primary focus was racing Siberian Huskies. If racing Siberians was being discussed anywhere in the world, the Norris name was probably in the conversation.

Two short, rather rotund people with graying hair stepped from the front door. Natalie had a warm, giggling chuckle to her speech. She reminded me of a female Santa. One-eyed Earl, on the other hand, scowled even when he laughed, a demonic, yet impish air about him. Earl was all-Alaskan—gritty, grizzled, and proud of it.

"Howdy, folks. Welcome to Willow," said Earl with his backwoods drawl.

"I just took an apple pie out of the oven. Come on in; the coffee's on," Natalie laughed. She loved to cook and loved to eat.

Debris littered the property. There were trucks, stripped chassis for training the dogs, antlers, skins, wires, wood, chain link fence for kennels, hundreds of empty, 50-pound sacks of dog food. Disorder reigned.

The house was crammed with memorabilia and "stuff." The walls were covered with photographs of Earl and Nat racing their dogs or receiving awards. The boys sat down at the long, cluttered dining room table and smiled at the prospect of an Alaskan-size slice of Natalie's famous pie as I craned my neck to look out over the largest dog lot in the world.

The brutal weather in the McKinley Range made flying into the Ruth Glacier impossible, so for many weeks the boys camped in Talkeetna and waited for a break in the weather. What unfolded as bad luck for them proved to be great fortune for me as I lived at Norris', treated like family—people always were. Earl owned one of the finest collections of first edition classics of the Pole Expeditions and Far North fiction in existence. I recovered rapidly, devouring book after book about the Arctic and Antarctic. I read until my vision doubled, caught up in the mystique of snow and ice, the Midnight Sun, the endless arctic nights, the wild animals of the North.

Reels of scratchy, 8mm film of Earl, Natalie, and the other famous competitors entertained me in the evenings. Weekly races were run on 10 to 25-mile courses set by snowmobiles—"sprint" races—and Earl had filmed many over the winters of their life. I was struck by how few women competed in the serious events. In fact, the few that did frequently used their husbands' or fathers' dogs. Natalie always trained and raced her own dogs, but she was retiring the coming winter. Earl let that fact drop early on. He also mentioned that while they frequently engaged several handlers, no one had applied for the following season. I got hopelessly sucked into the allure of sled dog racing. Before many weeks passed, I was desperate to become the Norris's handler. With my mindset that nothing was impossible, I also dreamed of taking over Natalie's second-string team and racing with the big boys.

As soon as my health allowed, I got to work. I needed to prove to Earl that I was strong and tough enough to labor long hours, manage a team, and survive the harshness of a musher's life. The three of us worked non-stop. Every dog had to be watered and fed, and every dog had to have his poop scooped daily. That became my job. My muscles screamed in rebellion each day as I pulled a plastic sled up and down the aisles of the entire dog farm, shoveling dog shit and hauling it out into a meadow and onto a fecal mountain. Earl refused to let me use a harness on myself to make the effort easier. But he'd finally found a name for me:

"How's the Pooper Scooper this morning?"

"The Pooper Scooper's lookin' purdy tired today."

"Ain't it amazing how heavy dog shit can be, Pooper Scooper?"

This guy was getting on my nerves. But my heart scanned the lots, tails wagged, dogs ran in circles around their houses, and I knew I would put up with anything to pass my initiation. No matter how long or hard I worked, Earl always had the next project waiting for me. Snide remarks peppered his every conversation with me. Earl was trying to break me. I danced a strange jig that year, shackled by the authority-figure issues my father had engendered, trying to become my own person in the shadow of Earl. I never met a man more difficult to stand up to than Earl Norris. Thank goodness Natalie was there to salve the emotional wounds he inflicted on me daily.

Eventually the boys climbed their mountain. Returning from Talkeetna, they sat around the dinner table eating moose steaks and talked about their feat. It was time for them to head south.

The next morning as they packed the Jeep, I caught Earl alone.

"Earl, I want to stay. I want to work for you. I promise you I will work day and night if only you will let me race next winter."

I hated begging, but I knew he would relish my subservience.

"Well, Pooper Scooper, I don't know. This is a purdy tough life. You think you got what it takes? Hereabouts winters run 40 below or worse. You'd be out there in the dark and cold, doing all the waterin', feedin', and cleanin', plus running lots of yearlings every day. And they'll eat you alive at the races — a young, inexperienced girly like you from the city. Think you're tough enough to *survive*?" His dead eye wept as he grinned meanly.

"Earl, I swear to you, I'll give you everything I've got. I know I can do this."

"OK, then. Let's give 'er a try. But don't come cryin' to me when you start to hurtin'. I'll begin ya with a three-dog team and see if ya can keep the sled upright. We'll take 'er from there."

The Willys pulled out as I waved goodbye to my friends, blowing kisses, hiding tears. My career as a sled dog racer began.

The Howling Dog Farm was the sled-dog hub of the world in those days. The old timers who had known Nat and Earl since the post-war era visited, and Eskimos and Athabaskans who left the bush for business in the big city stopped by to overnight. I thrived on those encounters. They meant that I got a break from my 14-hour, seven-day-a-week work schedule to come inside, drink coffee, and meet some of the most famous racers in the world as well as some of the most audacious characters in Alaska.

Whenever one of the natives took a liking to me, Earl teased me mercilessly: "You gonna be that musher's squaw? Think I'll call you squaw from now on." Squaw was the most derogatory name the men used for women in mushing circles.

Summer flew. We built new kennels for the puppies, repaired doghouses, checked every chain hook-up to make sure there were no weak links that would allow an unplanned mating. The sun dropped below the horizon but never set, so the urge to sleep diminished with the long days until I found myself going to bed at 1 a.m. and getting up at 5 a.m.

As I worked through the dog lot each day, I got to know the dogs. The males had glamorous Alaskan names: Nicolai, Tok, Nenana. The females were called by girls' names like Lucy and Peggy. I discovered the "shy" dogs (those too wild to be handled by Earl) allowed me to approach them, touch them, even harness them. Later the Pooper Scooper would be given all the shy year-olds to try to break into harness. I was never bitten.

The dogs howled up a storm and pranced and jumped off the ground with all four legs when I walked out the front door with the dog brush. I groomed as many as I could each day. Those animals spent their lives outside, chained to a doghouse, never given the attention of a house dog.

"What 'er you doin', treatin' those dogs like pets? Nobody treats dogs that way. You'll be the laughing stock of Alaska."

I ignored Earl, ordered a loom to spin dog wool, and collected copious amounts of undercoat during the summer. The dogs voted me the most popular dog handler they ever had. I came to love those animals as if each one was my child.

In autumn, we started training on dirt. Sometimes we took Earl's two-ton pickup to Hatcher Pass Road, which was originally the path along Willow Creek where the gold rush took place. We loaded about 25 dogs, drove to the bottom of the pass, hooked a gang line to the front of the truck, and snapped in harnesses on either side. Our leaders were put in first to hold the line out. We then worked our way back with the strongest (and often dumbest) dogs harnessed last, near the front bumper of the truck. The dogs went insane as we hooked them up, tugging in their harnesses, barking, yipping, and choking themselves with enthusiasm.

Earl started the pickup, the dogs lunged madly forward, and off we went. Once we gained momentum the team pulled us up the pass. Oh how those dogs loved to pull. That was a huge number of dogs to run at one time, considering the tangles, fights, or injuries that could occur while we were underway. If anything did go askew, I was the one who jumped from the truck, sped to the problem, and put it right. It wasn't just the dogs getting an endorphin rush on those wild training runs.

The other fall training method was even more daunting. Earl cut a narrow, circuitous trail on his homestead through dog-hair forests of lodgepole pine and dwarf spruce. Roots and ruts littered the course, and tree limbs stuck out precariously. We hooked up a team to a VW Bug chassis — four wheels, two seats, and a steering wheel — and flew through the bush, often unable to see the lead dogs around the bends. Hanging on, ducking all the dangers, and tending to the dogs made for a ride of bedlam. Earl roared with delight when he saw my fright. Of course, he braced against the steering wheel for stability while I struggled for all I was worth to stay on. We survived those training runs without any injuries to us or the four-leggeds.

Bright red corduroy all but jumped from its roll as I stood in the sewing store in downtown Anchorage. Natalie lent me an original, hand-drawn Eskimo parka pattern, and with wide-eyed anticipation, I picked out the materials to sew my very own parka on the industrial sewing machine we used to make the dogs' harnesses. This garment would protect me through the coldest winter nights, keep me alive if I lost my sled in the wilderness, be my racing jersey at the competitions. I wanted to pet the wolf ruff I chose to rim the hood. It broke my heart to think of the trapping and killing of wolves, yet I knew I needed that ruff to keep the winter air from freezing my lungs. Sewing the parka gave me deep respect for the elements and the risks I would face in the coming months.

One November morning I awoke to a shimmering white blanket covering the world. Winter had arrived.

My first team was comprised of three ancient dogs, just as Earl promised. Balancing on a sprint sled was tricky, even at slow speeds. But learn I did, until, at the onset of the race season, I was running between nine and 13 dogs. The winter was brutal, yet I loved every minute of my life.

I trained in the dark at 40 below. One night, flying down a trail, the team pointing at the full moon rising ahead, a snowy owl swooped right over my head and drifted along above my long team as they pounded over the snow with excited acceleration. That was the kind of magic only Alaska could conjure up.

Earl drove me into town to sign us up for the races. As we waited in line, he turned to me: "You 'magine you're good enough, girly, to race the "B" team? Yup, guess we'll give ya a try." My dream was coming true; I was taking Natalie's place with the "B" string, running with the best racers in the world. Except for my leader, Peggy, the dogs I trained were all pure Siberian Huskies. I was proud of my yearlings.

I grew strong and fat on Natalie's pie and love. I needed the blubber out there in the cold. My relationship with the dogs deepened. I now gave each dog a massage after a hard run, another source of guffawing from the male mushers: "Hey, squaw, I could use a massage myself right about now."

Thrashing in bed, exhausted from a sleepless night, I was sick with anxiety. The first big race of the season would begin in several hours; my day of reckoning was upon me. Mushers and spectators from all over the state were converging at the

Anchorage racetrack. While there were categories for kids, women with small teams, and juniors, I would race eleven dogs in the "A" category.

We pulled the dog-box trailer behind the big red truck, two canines to a box, nestled on beds of straw. No chatter ensued during the drive as Earl, Nat, and I considered the event to come. Were they worrying about my performance? I was.

Hundreds of people filled the parking lot as we pulled in and sought a place for a stakeout. Colorful banners flared, a loudspeaker screeched, kids with runny noses cried, looking for their lost parents. Dogs were staked out as far as I could see, making as much noise as teenagers at a rock concert. As I jumped to the snow from the high bench of the truck, all hell broke loose inside my bowels, my teeth chattered from nervousness, and my body trembled. I dashed to a Porta-Potty, fumbled with my heavy garments, and managed not to soil myself. I realized there was a big difference between running dogs in the wilderness and racing them in the midst of hordes of people, the most famous mushers in the sport, and the chaotic turmoil of hundreds of crazed huskies.

"Here's your start number, girly. The only woman in the big race. Now don't you go screw this up on me."

Natalie helped me pull the bib over my fat red parka and wished me luck. I was the ninth racer out, and my time was coming up way too quickly. I kicked my snow hook into the cement-hard snow of the parking lot to secure the sled, set out the line, attached the harnesses. The dogs went crazy with anticipation. When I unhooked Peggy and walked her to the front of the line, my team took command of the noise competition. The louder they got the more tense I became.

I quivered at the start line, sweat pouring from the pores of my face and instantly freezing. People stood on both sides of my team, holding the straining dogs back by their harnesses as I stood on the brake with my full weight. The race marshal counted "Three, two, one, go," and the team broke away with a rocket burst of speed.

The course undulated away from the populated area, took a left turn onto an eight-mile loop around a huge open space with forest off to musher's left. At the end of the loop, it turned left again back to the Start/Finish line. Racers were visible coming and going on the first mile and along the loop across the open space.

My excellent lead dog, Peggy, was a cross between a Siberian and a male Irish Setter Natalie kept as a pet behind the house. One day the Setter got loose while no one was home and had a ball out in the dog lot. Peggy was the champ of those litters. Her one problem: She was way too smart. She thought for herself. A successful racer wants a lead dog who follows all commands to perfection, yet regards the musher as the leader of the pack. In Peggy's case, she behaved as the alpha. My treating her like a person instead of a dog certainly had much to do with that dilemma. I was too inexperienced to realize it at the time.

I hawed Peggy onto the big loop. We were making great time. The fact that my team could smell and see other dogs excited them. When excited, they ran faster. The trail was superb, not rutted nor snaky, not icy nor too soft. My confidence slowly returned. In fact, I became downright cocky.

Gee, maybe I'll finish in the top ten. That would show Earl.

We were quite a distance out when the trail started to curve around to the right, then run straight again. Peggy pointed her Irish Setter nose over her right shoulder but kept running straight, holding the team well lined out. I couldn't figure out what she was looking at.

"Peggy, come on girl, pay attention up there."

The problem was, she *was* paying attention. She was eyeing in the far distance the place where the trail reentered the forest and headed back to the finish line. And she was thinking. She was thinking that a five-mile race would be better than 10 and that she could take a detour across the open meadows and frozen swamplands.

In one of the most harrowing moments of my life, Peggy darted off the trail onto snow hard enough to carry the teams' weight, drew the whole team behind her, and headed directly for the intersection. She knew the definition of a shortcut.

"Whoa, Peggy, whoa, goddammit. Peggy. Whoa, girl."

I balanced the sled while putting as much of my body weight onto the brake as possible. I dragged my other leg in the snow to further slow us down. The brake made a sharp, hissing noise, plowing a furrow, straight as an arrow toward the finish line. I slowed the team down for a moment, but they figured out that Peggy was taking them home and pulled again with all the force I had trained into them.

And then I saw it: A pipeline ran across the entire white vastness we were now crossing, perpendicular to our trajectory. It was maybe two feet in diameter and hid menacingly just under the snow. Jumping over pipelines was not in my training regimen.

The dogs bounded over the pipeline in graceful leaps, like well-trained ballerinas. I could feel the acceleration as they landed on the other side and dug in for the sprint home. When I reached the pipeline, I lifted the brush bow high in the air, elevated the sled, and slid it across the top of the pipe. I leaped, not a graceful ballerina. I landed on the far side and jumped on the runners, praying. Then my balance deserted me. In an instant I was being dragged, snow in my eyes, in my nose, in my mouth.

"Whoa, you damn dogs, whoa."

There was just no stopping them. But, if there was one thing in the world I knew, it was that I sure as hell was not going to let go of the sled. They could pull me all the way to the Arctic Circle, but I would come over that finish line with my team, whether upright or being dragged behind. I wondered whether my arms could be pulled from their sockets. Little black dots danced before my eyes. I held on.

A change in the snow brought me to my senses. We were back on the trail and moving slowly up a little hill. Now was my chance. I scrambled to my feet, twisted the sled upright, and stumbled onto the runners. I could barely stand up; my strength had left me.

A *whoosh* told me that we were on the downhill, and the dogs were sprinting again. A sharp, right-hand curve was coming up. There was a large conifer at the edge of the trail. I braced myself. The front half of the team went left around the tree; the back half went right; the sled careened toward the trunk. CRACK! The brush bow shattered. Then the main line broke in the middle, a seeming impossibility. I went down again.

Earl is going to take me out back and shoot me like a dog that has to be put down.

Peggy, freed when the line broke, took off with her four charges in a dash for the finish. As she vanished around the next bend, I could imagine the announcer telling the world that half a team of dogs was coming in without their sled and musher. Who could that musher be?

The six dogs I was still attached to struggled to get out of the tangle with the tree. They wanted to chase Peggy; they were having a hell of a good time. I jumped to my feet, righted the damaged sled, got it onto the trail, jumped on—and lost my balance one last time.

The announcer was shouting wildly into the microphone, his voice echoing through the forest. The racing community had never seen a team bisected, finishing in two parts. Nor had they ever heard of anyone being dragged that far. I crossed the finish line, sled badly battered, but not as battered as my bloody body and pummeled pride. The rear half of my team had hauled me all the way back on my belly.

I learned lessons that day. I realized that my inexperience played a role; I forgave myself that inexperience. As the season passed, I watched men who mushed their whole lives get into serous predicaments; it was part of the sport. I hadn't let go, and that was something to be really proud of.

While I was no competition for the world-class guys, I did well for myself that winter. It took about a month to recover from the dragging. Seems I should have been in a full-body cast. Earl did not fire me, but I did rightfully pay for the repairs to the sled. He paid me all the race money I won. At the Willow Winter Carnival, I passed the World Champion, George Attla, a native from the bush, as he stood on the side of the trail, his dogs in a big tangle. Because I bested him that day—a woman, a city girl, a *cheechako* (tenderfoot)—he never spoke to me again. In the three-day Women's World Championships, I finished fifth. The women ahead of me had all raced since childhood, running their families' "A" teams for the event. I ran Peggy and my yearlings.

The inaugural Iditarod started that spring. Willow is now the official host of the actual race start.

In the following years, Rocky, Neils, and Johnny died climbing in the mountains. Only dear, sweet Frank survives.

A renowned female musher, Susan Butcher, handled her dogs with the same loving care and training philosophy that I embraced. She won the Iditarod three times. I felt vindicated. Later, while living in Switzerland, a handsome young Swiss, Martine Buser, asked me to write him a letter of recommendation to the Norrises. He handled for them, became a renowned racer in his own right, and won the Iditarod three times.

Nat and Earl were married 55 years. Earl died in 2001. They left a legacy that will forever endure, influencing many lives, including mine, in a profound and unforgettable way.

Chapter 4

GOING TO THE DOGS

Alaska, The End of Winter, 1973

"You have power over your mind… Realize this, and you will find strength."

~ Marcus Aurelius

The State of Alaska was both a modern world and a place out of time. Men dwelled in the wilderness, living like the miners and trappers of bygone centuries, without communication with the outside world, without modern conveniences, without women. One day, I found myself in their world.

Working seven days a week in the cold and dark all winter had taken its toll. When Joey Schmitt came to visit, I was so ready to escape the Farm, I would have left with anyone. Joey was the penultimate redneck and sprinkled his backwoods slang with lots of "ain'ts" and "shits." A matchstick was usually balanced on his lower lip, and his scraggly beard was punctuated with ice and, occasionally, snot. Tall and beefy, he sported patched and ripe clothing. He had seen me from afar at several races and got it into his head that I was attracted to him and that he should whisk me away for a weekend adventure.

The Schmitt family — Joey, his brother, and his dad — lived in the true Alaskan wilderness. They owned a lodge built during the gold rush in the unpopulated interior. As many as 3,000 "road houses" existed in Alaska and the Yukon during those pioneer days. It is hard to define "roadhouse" because those establishments ranged from dug-outs to two-story luxury log structures. Roadhouses provided food and shelter for prospectors seeking their fortune and are counted among the most colorful institutions in Alaska's history.

The Schmitt's place was accessible in winter only by dog sled or snowmobile. When the snow melted, hunters made their way in over the rugged terrain with four-wheel drive vehicles. The Schmitt men earned a living by housing sportsmen during the hunting season and spent the rest of the year as trappers.

"So, Barbara," said Joey, "if you say yes, we can meet my brother on the highway. He's supposed to pick me and the supplies up on Tuesday. We'll pack you in on the sled with the food. Think how nice and comfy you'll be under a bunch of bearskins. Jake and I can stand together on the runners. I'll take you to a place so remote and beauteous, you could never imagine it in your wildest dreams. Now ain't that the best offer you got this winter? Say yes, girl."

"Earl, I want to go up to Schmitt's place over the weekend with Joey. I need a break badly."

"You think that's safe, being alone with those three crazies out thar in the wilderness? You'd better think agin, girly."

I weighed Earl's words. Yes, Joey was unschooled and uncouth, but he seemed like a nice enough guy. I figured Earl was yanking my chain as usual and would make it as hard for me to go as he could without tying me to a doghouse.

I approached the invitation with a distinct innocence, a psyche that had no preparedness for the danger of men. Sixteen years of Catholic school hadn't taught me about people like Joey.

While the girls at my convent college experimented with sex, I was imploring the Blessed Virgin to keep me from the temptation of *thinking* about sex. I had grown up in a family so sheltered from the realities of life that it never occurred to me to consider my vulnerability.

I told Joey to pick me up on his way home.

Joey pulled his truck off the icy road into a plowed pullout and left the engine running with the heater on high as we waited for his brother to show up on the dogsled. We watched the colossal hulk of Mt. McKinley in silence as its snow plume blew like a long, vaporous flag. The temperature outside hovered around 30 below. Taking off into the bush with trappers on a freight sled promised a thrilling adventure into the primitive past.

Jake mushed out of the dwarfed forest on the long runners of a huge sled pulled by eight enormous, mangy dogs. I couldn't make out his face well because the wolf ruff around his parka hood concealed it, but I could tell that his burly beard and eyelashes were iced over. He looked like a giant in his big parka and Navy-issue arctic bunny boots. We jumped from the truck and loaded supplies into the sled. The hairs in my nostrils instantly froze; my eyes burned with the cold. Although my parka hood covered my head and most of my face, I breathed through my nose, not my mouth, to protect my lungs.

I waited for Joey to make an introduction. None was forthcoming.

Before long I was bouncing painfully down a rutted trail in the sled, snuggled in fur but still freezing. As the short, sub-arctic day waned, the temperature continued to drop. We wove our way ever deeper into the wilderness. It was dead still, the silence mysterious and unearthly. A white ice cloud hovered above the team from the dogs' breath. As we topped a ridge, McKinley appeared so near that I felt I could reach out and touch it. That majestic mountain seen in the faltering rays of the day's light became engraved on my heart. As we mushed on, I pondered whether life at the lodge would be like living in an earlier century. I sure hoped so.

After numbing hours in the sled, it was a shock to come around a bend at dusk and see a large, two-story structure built of massive tree trunks. Several sheds filled the open space. Junk stretched to the boundaries of the ancient forest—parts of snowmobiles, broken tools, trapping rigs, pick axes, oil cans. Carcasses of everything from huge moose to little martens, Alaska's most trapped animal, lay in the blood-stained snow where the Schmitts butchered them.

Joey's racing-dog lot was situated on the south side of the dwelling to protect the dogs from the northerly winds barreling down from the McKinley Range. The dogs in the lot made a racket. They sensed and smelled something new: me.

Joey's dad, Hank, came to the door.

"Hey, Pa. This is Barbara, up from Earl and Nat's."

Pa was soused and burped several times in a crude greeting. He matched his sons' height; his girth spoke to the many cases of beer he consumed over the dark winter. He was as silent as Jake, but seemed a friendly drunk.

The bottom floor of the lodge was a huge room with rafters made of mighty beams and a fireplace constructed with giant river rocks. The floorboards were well worn from the era when many men used the roadhouse for food, shelter, and community. Three worn couches faced the fireplace in a U. Hides covered the walls—bear, moose, elk, wolf. I wondered about the people who sought refuge in this place, what sorts of rugged, lonely men had lived and died there. I wondered if a woman had ever stepped foot inside.

The room would have been beautiful except for the hundreds of beaver testicles that hung from the rafters. There were hides from other animals, but the beaver balls really caught my attention. I found the carnage bedecking the great room bizarre and upsetting.

"Joey, what in the world are those things doing up there in the rafters?"

"Oh, yah, well, they need to dry out. There's a good market for 'em. Guess some folk think they're a potent aphrodeeeziac. Takes all kinds. Course, I don't need no aphrodeeeziac. No ma'am."

We ate a dinner of bear stew. The men were so reserved and strange that I wondered if they were the product of inbreeding. They spoke a bit about their trap lines to one another. The Schmitts were too busy drinking to engage in conversation with me. I wanted to know about the history of the lodge. Surely the roadhouse held remarkable stories from the past: When was the lodge built, by whom, what route was the lodge on, was gold found here? I learned nothing.

There was no alcohol at the Howling Dog Farm. Here, for every beer I had, they drank three apiece. Between the lack of practice, the dehydration from the sled trip, and the fatigue from the cold, it didn't take long for me to develop a rosy-cheeked buzz.

After dinner, Jake and Hank rejected my offer to help clean up and vanished into the kitchen. I found myself alone in front of a roaring fire with Joey, who was by then pretty much bombed out of his mind. I was startled by a sudden, piercing chorus of wails.

"What's that sound?"

"Damn wolves. Howl up a storm every night. We got a pack hangs round the place all winter. Guess they're smellin' the kills from our trap lines and the dogs, 'course."

"Oh, please, can we grab our parkas and go out and listen?"

"You gotta be kidding. It's probably 60 below out there by now. Why would you want to ruin such a warm, relaxed evenin' like that?

"Because I have never in my life heard a pack of wolves in the dead of night at 60 below. I'll go out alone, if you won't come with me."

The moon hung above the hills to the south. It lit the still, white land and made it shimmer. The wolves must have been on the last ridge we'd come over with the freight sled, very close at hand. I thrilled to the sound of their lamenting chorus.

"Had enough yet? I'm freezing my butt off out here. Let's go get another beer."

Our brief outdoor excursion sobered Joey up enough to make him want to drink more. My head was clearing, and I began to worry about this stranger who was getting increasingly hammered.

"So Joey, where do I sleep?"

"Oh. We're gonna sleep upstairs in the big bunkroom. I usually sleep in the bedroom with Jake, which is warmer, but figured we'd want a little privacy. Wanna see it?"

With lantern in hand, he led me up a flight of stairs, bowed by 100 years of wear. 20 or so beds, each topped with a stained pillow and several smelly blankets, filled the freezing bunkroom. Joey sat on a bed and stroked the space beside him. The lantern cast foreboding shadows. Dark spaces beyond the light seemed to harbor the ghouls and ghosts of an era past.

"Come on over here, honey. Let me warm you up."

I stood above him and said as calmly as I could: "Look, Joey, I never said anything about sex. I don't even know you."

"Ah, you're just toyin' with me. Come here, sugar."

"No way. Forget it, Joey."

"Now you're flaunting yourself at me, darlin'. I can see you askin' for it."

Someplace in the back of my consciousness, I knew that the trip had been building to this moment and realized that I had suppressed the idea in order to make the journey. But now I could no longer deny what was happening and grew tremulous.

If I scream and bring the other two drunks up here, I could be facing a gang bang.

Joey grabbed both my hands, pulled me down to the bed, and landed on top of me so deftly that I wondered how he could be the same uncoordinated drunk I watched mount the stairs. His clothes stunk of dirt, sweat, and urine. His greasy hair sickened me. I was buried in his stench.

He threaded his fingers through my hair and held my head in a vice grip. His other hand began to grope, caressing me roughly. His tongue, like a venomous snake, thrust into my mouth. The taste of chew and beer on his breath made me gag. I was sure I would puke all over him; I wished I *could* puke all over him.

And then a miracle occurred. A core strength arose in me that I had never before experienced around men. My sense of helplessness vanished. I began to feel *entitled* to defend myself. My gut told me that I could escape this predicament. There was no reasoning to my thoughts, only the certainty that I could and would protect myself.

We battled—first on the creaking, malodorous bed, then rolling off onto the hard, dusty floor.

"No!" I screamed.

Tears streamed down my face while I hit, punched, and clawed at him with the considerable strength I had developed working the dogs. Adrenaline bolstered my power to fight back.

"Get off of me," I demanded.

And then I did something I'd only seen in movies: I kicked him in the crotch with all the force I could muster.

"That's for me and all those poor beavers, you shithead."

He rolled onto his side in agony, legs drawn up to his stomach. "You bitch. You little bitch," he groaned.

I took a stand and looked around wildly for something to use as a weapon. There was nothing.

A very angry man rose from the floor. He stared at me drunkenly and said:

"So you don't want to make hanky panky with Joey? Maybe you want to fuck around with my dogs instead? Let's just take this little lady outside and throw her to the dogs. They'll tear you to pieces, bitch. Let's see how you like that."

Joey scooped me up, threw me over his shoulder and headed down the stairs. I shrieked and screamed, battered his back with my fists. I felt like a rabbit in the jaws of a grizzly bear. We were out the door and into the frigid night within seconds.

It was so very cold.

Joey staggered toward the dog lot, calling to his huskies:

"Hey boys, lookee what I got here. Want a piece of ass?"

His hollering and my screaming incensed the dogs. They jerked on their chains, snarling, shrieking, and snapping; the dog lot became a madhouse.

"Joey, *please* don't do this."

White canines flashed in the moonlight. I bent my knees and wrapped my legs around his waist to keep away from the lunging dogs as he paraded me through the lot.

"Don't drop me. Do not drop me, Joey."

"Hey dawgs. Got me a wild one here. Want some of her? Fine legs, cute bottom," he chortled as he tottered between the doghouses. He reached back and slapped my rear end hard. Icy tears froze on my face. I could fight the man, but I couldn't fight a lot full of crazed dogs.

"Gee, it's fr', fr', freezing out here," he suddenly stuttered to himself as the glacial temperatures started to sober him up.

"Joey, let's go back inside. It's too cold to be out here. This is insane."

The arctic night saved my life. He stumbled from the mania of the dog lot with me still over his shoulder and mumbled about how cold he was. When we reached the front door, he dropped me like a big sack of dried dog food. Paralyzed by cold and dread, my legs failed me. I collapsed onto the snow and curled into a fetal position, trembling in disbelief at the fate I barely escaped.

"Aw, come on now, can't you take a joke, girl? Here, let me help you up."

Joey passed out on the couch in front of the dying fire as soon as we got inside. I dragged myself up the stairs and wrapped myself in blankets, too horrified to sleep.

In the morning, three gamey, hung over males sat at the breakfast table drinking a nasty version of what they called coffee.

With authority, I demanded: "I want to go back *now*."

"I'll git the snowmobile up and runnin' and take you out," Joey said flatly.

So ended my holiday from the Howling Dog Farm. I couldn't wait to get back. Hard work and dog shit never looked so good.

Over time, fire destroyed many of Alaska's famed roadhouses. Nature and neglect claimed most of the remainder. Fortunately, some survived in the proximity of civilization, were restored and serve today as reminders of a rugged past. They are now mainly bed and breakfasts, resorts, hunting lodges or hotels. They offer guests a genuine experience of life in the pioneer days with antique furnishings, historic accoutrements like bear traps and five-foot long snowshoes as well as sled dog memorabilia.

In addition, some provide gourmet cooking, snowmobile rides in winter, four wheeler rides in

summer, and chances to pan for gold on a nearby creek — an immersion into the era of the gold rush with all the conveniences of modernity.

Of that roadhouse in the wilderness and the men who dwelled there, I know nothing more. One visit was enough for a lifetime.

Chapter 5

THE ROAD FAR LESS TRAVELED

India to Nepal, 1976

"What lies behind us and what lies before us are tiny in comparison to what lies within us."
~ *Ralph Waldo Emerson*

The train rattled and creaked its way north into the night. As usual, my budget permitted only third class travel with the masses, but that was the way I liked it, down and dirty. Calcutta was far behind me now. The lingering scent of the travelers and the barnyard smell of their animals were all that remained of a long, stifling day. Images of the poor, rural Indian life I saw out the window reflected in my mind.

In typical travel-safety fashion, I draped my upper body over my grungy, red backpack and tried to rest. The discomfort of the hard, wooden seat and the grating sound of the old train made sleep elusive. I worried about the outcome of yesterday's efforts to secure a border permit that would get me into the exotic reaches of the northern provinces. What would happen if my plans failed?

I had become a gypsy; I wandered the world. I had no home, no belongings other than the clothes in my backpack, no community, nothing binding me to any person or place. My passport opened like a travel brochure with extended pages to allow for its many stamps. This lifestyle seemed more natural to me than my upbringing in New York ever had.

My newest journey started in Amritsar, the golden capitol of Sikhdom, on the western border of India. Tibet was my dream destination, but the Chinese shut it down tight, so ultimately I planned to trek alone through Nepal and investigate not only Nepalese life, but Buddhist culture as well. Between Amritsar and Nepal worlds of adventure called to me.

I traveled east, crossed the subcontinent by train and eventually landed in Calcutta, the most heart-wrenching city I had seen on the planet. Other than the rare white tigers with their flashing azure eyes at the zoo, Calcutta offered nothing but tears and sorrow. Naked, living skeletons lay dying in the streets. The suffering of Calcutta, contrasted with the grandeur of the buildings and parks of the earlier British Empire, was unbearable. I outlined my escape from the "City of Pain" with eager desperation.

I looked north to Darjeeling and Sikkim with their awe-inspiring views. Hindi, Sikkimese (Bhutia), Tibetan, Lepeha, and Limboo were spoken in Sikkim. The diversity of peoples and the splendor of the mountains called to me. Climbing led me to read many books about that part of the world. Images of dense jungles, barren high plains, raging rivers, and sky-ripping peaks mesmerized me.

As I reviewed my primitive map of the regions bordering Tibet, how could I not dream of Bhutan, the Hidden Kingdom, the reputed land of Shangri-La. My travel book said the government barred travelers from entering. As a child I'd seen the 1930's movie Hollywood made about this kingdom. The *quest* for a place of immeasurable beauty and ultimate peace captured my heart all those years ago. I reasoned, once I reached Sikkim, perhaps I'd find a way to sneak into Bhutan and discover my own paradise. Lots of magical thinking there. Let's blame it on Hollywood.

Darjeeling and Sikkim required a visa. I showed up at the government permit office in Calcutta at the official opening time and received my first foul taste of Indian bureaucracy. Since this was an office for any and all permits and since India was prone to requiring permits for anything and everything, the place was swamped. A line of citified Hindus as wide as the sidewalk ran the length of the block and around the corner. There were only men in the line, short and dark with piercing black eyes. Most carried an umbrella, some a briefcase. They seemed indifferent to the heat and the agonizing wait. I spent the day in that queue with the stench of the street in my nostrils, the humidity dizzying in its intensity.

At 4 p.m., just as I reached the desk of the clerk who would control my destiny, the few people ahead of me walked off. I ran to the clerk.

"Sir, Sir! I must get a permit today for Darjeeling and Sikkim. I've been in line since 9 a.m. Please, help me!"

A six-day Hindu holiday began that evening and the government offices would be shut during the festival. I couldn't bear to spend another day in Calcutta, much less another week. I dug rapidly for a little bribe, my only hope of keeping him there long enough to issue my permits. He wasn't interested.

"Sorry, Missie, but the office is closed now. Come back in one week," he said, head bobbing in that strange Indian fashion.

"No, please, sir, isn't there some other way to get my permits? Can I get them at the border?"

The little rat told me I could.

I hurried back to my comfortable, colonial-inspired room at the YMCA, packed my few belongings, and rushed to catch the night train. As it headed north, relief at escaping Calcutta mingled with a slight concern that the civil servant was wrong about the border. I should have had more than a slight concern.

---

600 miles later the train came to an abrupt and final halt. The few passengers I traveled with that day exited and disappeared into the dark, dense jungle. I stepped off the train; it was early morning. A steady drone of insects emanated from the tropical forest. The earth smelled of rotting vegetation, a surprisingly rich, pleasant odor. I was standing on the cracked platform of an ancient British railway station. I knew that I had left Calcutta in 1974 and had just reached the border of Darjeeling. But which century had I landed in?

A guard in full dress uniform — *cum* rifle — was marching formally in my direction. He looked like a nasty gurkha out of a Rudyard Kipling novel. His rigid face and stiff demeanor scared the shit out of me. Where had he come from? There was nothing there; no village, no roads that I could see. I found myself wondering how his uniform could be wrinkle-free in a climate with 100% humidity.

In proper Queen's English, he demanded my permit. I politely explained that the bureaucrat in Calcutta said I could acquire my visa at the border.

"That is thoroughly impossible, Missie. That would be against all regulations."

Tears welling, I asked, "What am I going to do?"

He informed me that I had to return to Calcutta, get my permit at the end of the Hindu holiday, and make the trip north a second time.

"Don't I have *any* other options?" I queried with annoyance. My insolence ticked him off. His cold indifference turned to anger.

"Yes you do, Missie. You can wait in the jail cell in the basement of this station with the rats for the next ten days until the magistrate comes through on his rounds. He can consider your case then."

A long silence ensued as I worried that he would march me with his rifle down the dark, dungeon stairs cut into the platform. My knees felt weak; my pack suddenly seemed to be loaded with bricks. I struggled for breath as internal tremors vibrated my limbs.

This must be what a panic attack feels like.

I wracked my brain for another option.

"Is there another train leaving here that doesn't go back to Calcutta but doesn't require a permit," I asked with a great deal more politeness.

He explained the dubious solution to me: A train traveled to and then along the river that formed the border with Nepal. I could take that train, disembark in the middle of nowhere, hike through the jungle to the border, and cross into Nepal. It only came through once a week, but it was my lucky day — it arrived at this end-of-the-world border station in just a few hours, around noon.

I looked at my simplistic map. It showed *nothing* in the southeastern corner of Nepal, and I said as much. He pointed to a blank spot, which became a sweaty finger print on my map, as he told me that I could follow a path to a tiny village on the Nepalese side.

"If you walk fast, Missie, you can arrive before dark. You had better move quickly. You don't want to be caught in the jungle at night."

He spoke in an authoritative voice. I hated him for his rigidity and his condescension. I decided he wanted me to be trapped out there in the darkness. My defiance pushed me over the edge of good sense, and my addiction to the thrill of menace blocked sane decision making.

And so it was that I left my original, crazy plans behind and crafted new ones as circumstance dictated. The railway was an antiquated line built by the British to the outstations of northern India in the colonial days. A toy engine pulled a single baby car on a narrow-gauge rail. The guard had explained my unusual plan to the train attendant so that he knew where in the wilderness to deposit me.

Within seconds of leaving the border station, dense jungle enveloped the mini train. The day became hotter by the minute; sweat saturated my clothes and dripped from my chin. Occasionally, monkeys darted about in the high branches, screeching at the sound of the engine. The hours passed in a blur of phosphorescent greens. The train chugged merrily enough through the jungle and stopped on command to drop off or pick up dark-skinned people who lived in primitive villages I never saw. They stared at me blankly as if a white face hadn't been seen on the line since the British built it. I strongly suspected that was true. Striking up a conversation with the shy attendant, I discovered that, indeed, he had *never* seen a tourist traveling that route.

He explained: "It doesn't go anywhere."

The day ended; the train halted. It was empty of passengers. Where was I and what was going on? We had stopped at a colonial bush station with a "guest house" attached. It had clearly not been used in a century; the walls were crumbling, the door missing. What beasts of the jungle would roam the room at night? I was directed inside. There were antique beds with mattresses and mosquito netting. Thick spider webs blanketed the ceiling. The attendant informed me that we would be departing at 6 a.m. sharp.

We're going to overnight here? Well, that seems pretty exotic too.

I didn't know where the engineer or the attendant slept, but I had the room to myself. I tried to choose the bed that seemed to have the least number of holes rotted into the protective netting, climbing onto a mattress well chewed by mice or rats.

The guard said nothing of a two-day journey. What if everything he told me was bogus?

I fell into a dazed, exhausted sleep.

I woke at dawn to discover that the "protective" fabric was badly decayed. There were more mosquitoes inside the drapes than out. I was covered in welts from head to toe. I prayed malaria would not be the awful price I would pay for the decision to take off into the unknown.

My second day of traveling began. The little train moved deeper into a world I knew few Westerners had ever seen. A person got on and off from time to time, but I saw no signs of civilization. About six hours later the train stopped, but no one had hailed it. My stop had arrived. I looked incredulously out into the wilderness. There was nothing but the vaguest hint of a trail leading into tall grasses. "This way, yes, this way, *memsab*," said the attendant, pointing into the nowhere.

And then the train slipped away, its chug, chug, chug rapidly fading into stillness. I stood there in shock, a hapless woman.

Is it suicidal to live like this? Just how alienated have I become? Why do I land myself in these situations over and over again? How ironic is it that I felt equally alone growing up on Long Island?

A bird squawked; I just about jumped out of my skin. A sense of tangible dread trickled down my back with my sweat.

Could this trail without a single footprint possibly deliver me to Nepal?

As I slung my pack over my shoulders and began to walk, more questions, like dark clouds in a building monsoon, troubled me. Would I make it to this village by nightfall? What if the trail simply petered out? I didn't even have a compass, but then I didn't know which direction would take me to the border. What about the dangers of venomous snakes and spiders? Perhaps woman-eating tigers inhabited the god-forsaken place since there was no one there to hunt them. And what other killer animals lived on that flat plain below the Himalayas — leopards, rhinoceros, wild boar, even elephants? My resolve frayed like the strands of a rotten rope coming unraveled.

My mind rambled on as I trekked along hour after agonizing hour:

If there is a border crossing, will they let me through? If there isn't, what will happen when I try to leave Nepal without an entry stamp?

Every sharp, hidden noise sent a jolt of adrenaline through my system like a lightening bolt. The jungle's sounds were my constant companion. Birds and bands of monkeys shouted alarm as I passed, and millions of insects droned incessantly. A primordial feeling shrieked a warning of claws and fangs lurking in the still grasses and smothering trees. Hideous spider webs spanned the forest. I didn't know whether to look down at the ground or up into the branches, but knew I had to remain on high alert. The jungle was a world of shadows with the rare beam of light piercing the thick canopy. Sometimes the forest would defer to open regions of high grass so tall that it came up to my armpits. I prayed not to lose my faint link to Nepal when the trail all but vanished again and again in those grasslands. The game I played as a child came to mind: Find the hidden animals in the picture of the jungle. The game was no longer fun.

I judged I had about two hours of daylight left. Apprehension of being stranded at night grew as the light shifted toward shades of evening. I sensed a general, cool dampening in the air and underfoot. The vegetation became greener; moss grew on the trees. Then I spotted a river. Well, it wasn't exactly a river;

it was more of a swampy stream swirling around tall grasses, buzzing with mosquitoes.

Are there crocodiles in the jungles of northern India?

A downed tree made for a bridge of sorts, and someone had placed primitive boards through the swamp for better footing. Someone besides me had at some point been there. Hope!

I lifted my gaze to the other side of the waterway. I thought I saw an outhouse. I crossed, balancing precariously on the log and boards, watched for the alligators and headed for the structure. It was the shape and size of an outhouse but looked to be an out-of-use, decaying shelter for, yes, a border crossing. I took a big step forward on the evasive trail and declared myself in Nepal, country of great and glorious Himalayan peaks, home of the snow leopard, land of my heart.

I picked up my pace, keenly aware of the low sun angle. Less than an hour later the sweet smell of smoke tickled my nose. The trail became wider; a tiny village appeared. 25 or 30 bamboo shacks surrounded a whitewashed colonial building with a flagpole decorating its front yard. Villagers moved about casually among dogs, pigs, chickens, and lots of playful, giggling kids.

One of the children, a tiny girl in rags with black, dusty hair tied in braids, spotted me. I must have scared her, coming out of the jungle like that, a Caucasian apparition. I looked straight into her eyes; they were big, black O's. Barefoot, she kicked up her little heels and fled. I moved in the direction of the official-looking building. A moment later I her saw her again, followed by the entire village. This was one exciting event for a community cut off from the world. No one was more excited than I.

It became immediately obvious that none of the villagers spoke English, but sign language worked like a charm. I was led to the white colonial-looking structure where the mayor lived with his family. To my delight, he spoke excellent English, having been educated by the British. He greeted me formally, yet cordially, and invited me to tea (Darjeeling, of course). Our teatime was quite civilized and contrasted dramatically with the simple life of the town. What a thrilling end to an adventurous day. And what a relief.

My gracious host explained that his village was the terminus of a "highway" which ran from east to west across Nepal, the Mahendra Highway. Most of the road was dirt, sometimes deeply rutted, sometimes a mud track, often impassable. Between the village and Kathmandu, two great rivers raged down gorges from the incomparable vastness of snow and ice that is the Himalaya. A one-lane bridge, he told me proudly, spanned the river nearer to the capitol. The other, however, was crossed by some sort of ferry.

He took me out to show me the bus station. The villagers followed, craning their necks to catch another view of the crazy white woman from the jungle. I wanted to spend more time with them, but the once-a-week bus was making its way east the following morning. There were no cars in eastern Nepal back then, so I decided I had better be on that bus if I wanted to get to Kathmandu anytime soon. I was graciously offered a meal with the mayor's family and a mat for sleeping in the study.

In the morning, every last inhabitant showed up to see me off. They treated our encounter as a great honor; I knew the privilege was mine.

———————

I waved good-bye to my newfound friends, a whole village, and began a long, exciting, and beautiful journey westward. The Mahendra Highway paralleled the southern border of the country at first, then headed northwest. To the south were the tropical jungles of India, to the north the highest and most dramatic peaks in the world. For the most part, the foothills blocked the glistening glaciers and sky-piercing summits, but my climber's heart knew I was near, and I was filled with joy to think that Mt. Everest was there in the clouds looking down upon me.

The bumpy, dirt road was adorned with brilliant, tropical flowers. Loud monkeys whooped in the trees in response to the appearance of the dilapidated bus. On the higher stretches of the road, the landscape changed to glorious, green bamboo forests. I saw no signs of huts, but people appeared along the way to wave down the bus. Another lesson in the meaning of "remote."

About three in the afternoon the driver stopped the bus, made a three-point turn, and opened the door. The villagers piled out with all their belongings. A bus waited for us on the other side of a river. A massive volume of water rushing furiously from the mountains above undercut the river's banks. Five distinct torrents poured out of the glaciers upriver, converging into the great waterway we had to cross. The khaki water, tinted by a combination of glacial silt and mud, raged before us, a pewter sheen ominously coloring its crashing waves.

An enormous dugout canoe sat on the bank's edge.

Our coffin to the other side, I thought as I stood in disbelief, looking at our "ferry."

It seemed impossible to take all these people across the undulating river in such a boat. The driver of the bus was also our ferryman. With the help of several of the men, he steadied the dugout in a powerful eddy, clutching a long pole that appeared useless for steering a reamed-out tree trunk through the surging mayhem.

The other passengers were no happier than I was about this crossing: I saw it in their faces. I wondered how often the boat capsized and everyone drowned. When the boat was loaded with passengers and luggage, it sat barely above the water level. I dubiously stepped into the water, handed my backpack into the dugout, and was pulled aboard, the last person to enter.

The little man in charge of our fate pushed off with his long pole. The torrent caught us instantly. We flew down the monstrous waves, rocking from side to side, threatened within seconds with swamping. We were on an aqueous rollercoaster ride. We shot a good 100 yards downriver.

If we don't drown before we reach the other side, we'll end up in the Indian Ocean.

Wailing pierced the air as water pounded against the canoe. People prayed, their palms pressed together and raised above their bowed heads. They either squeezed their eyes tightly shut or gazed up at the heavens. A few women shrieked at the tops of their lungs. It was understandable—I was holding back a cry of terror myself. The watery violence stripped me of any sense of control and all sense of safety. We tore down the vicious flow, slowly angling across, bobbing up and down like a cork. The river bellowed, sounds cracking like thunder from its depths.

This is insane. How will we ever get across?

But get to the other side we did—a miracle in my book. The boatman steered us into a large, roiling eddy with a small pebbled beach. A few of the men jumped from the bow and dragged the boat toward the shoreline, assisted by our Kathmandu bus driver. Everyone, including me, was wild-eyed with adrenaline. I understood then why most of the people of the village remained in their isolated world.

I walked with jelly legs back upriver to the next bus and had a good look at the dynamics of the fearsome river. Good thing there was a bridge for the second crossing. Neither my mind nor my body were willing to endure a repeat performance.

Halfway to Kathmandu we stopped at a primitive village for the night. I couldn't communicate with these natives either, but they welcomed me, offered me food, and treated me with a touching generosity. The shy children hid behind their mothers' skirts; the adults smiled unconditionally.

My traveling companions threw their bundles to the ground and concocted beds of blankets. I was honored with the only bed in town—a wooden, plank table. I anticipated that sleeping on those elevated boards would keep me bug-free, but I awoke at dawn in severe discomfort. My body was covered with little, red, itchy splotches. That night the feast on the villagers' table was my poor body.

The next day was as beautiful as the one before. The dusty, yellow bus gained and lost significant elevation as it wound through the Nepalese foothills. Reaching the second great river crossing, I thanked the gods heartily that a rickety bridge allowed us an easier passage. As a dramatic, mauve, Himalayan sunset lit the sky, the bus navigated steep paved switchbacks down into Kathmandu where an exotic, ancient civilization awaited me.

Now the Mahendra Highway is fully paved. Bridges span all the great rivers that it intersects in its journey across the country. The provinces of northeastern India advertise on the Internet. Even Bhutan, the last mysterious realm on earth, has been opened to tourism.

A simple offering of Baksheesh (a bribe) would have assured me a visa at the border, but I am happy that I chose to venture into a remote world of which I knew nothing. Sadly, that world has been replaced by adventure travel and the tourist dollar. The dangers and uncertainties of my journey were many, but addressing them helped me to learn more about the woman I was becoming.

Chapter 6

WANDERINGS IN NEPAL

Nepal, 1976

*"Travel is an agent for rebirth; I was being reborn
again and again."*
~ *Richard Bangs*

Chomolungma. The Mother Goddess Who Lives at the Top of the World. A tangible manifestation of the divine: Mount Everest.

I was in Nepal, and I was a climber. I had read every book written about the planet's highest mountain. It held a mystique far beyond any other mountain. Reigning over the glorious peaks of the Himalaya, it drew me like a spring draws animals to drink in the desert.

Yet I knew that I would never climb Everest. I had proven myself unworthy of such a lofty undertaking with my poor snow skills and near-fatal accidents. I would never approach the behemoth with crampons and ice axe in tow. I would have to find another way to experience the magnificence of the Great Mother Goddess.

A striking city, exhilarating and unfamiliar, flamboyant Kathmandu basked in a balmy subtropical valley, yet sat within a heartbeat of the pearly string of the highest, most formidable mountains on earth. Buddhist prayer flags swirled from shrines and rooftops, the ubiquitous laughter of children rang out in the markets, monks in gold or burgundy robes, heads shaven, floated through the sun-drenched streets.

The striking dress and dazzling jewelry of the women, even the poorest, surprised me. Gold was abundant; agate, amber, coral, glass, and turquoise beads decorated attire. The women wore dramatic pieces of adornment to celebrate marriage, promote fertility, and ward off evil spirits.

I searched out the mysteries of the great Hindu and Buddhist shrines. Lines of Nepalis and Tibetans, both locals and pilgrims, circumambulated the sanctuaries and reverently spun prayer wheels. The tinkling of countless bicycle bells complemented the sound of chanting which filled the air like a soft murmuring of cicadas in the jungle. The great stupa of Bodhanath, one of the most sacred sights, exuded spiritual force; the all-seeing eyes of the supreme Buddha cast their gazes in the cardinal directions.

Kathmandu's temples beguiled me; peacefulness, spirituality, and ethereal energy filled each one, their butter lamps flickering a bright message of compassion and peace to the planet. I wanted to visit all 2,700 of them!

In my travels, I was beginning to discover the sense of the unseen side of being, of life beyond life. Here, I could feel the holiness in these temple sectors. In a place overflowing with primitive commerce, noise, and exotic scents, a sense of the mystical pervaded the commonplace. Had I not wanted to explore, I could have settled in Kathmandu with its salubrious climate for an extended period of time and allowed the spiritual side of my being to be nurtured by the mind stream of the environment.

But exploration was paramount. I could never get enough of the newness, the freshness, and the beauty of such worlds. I wasn't going to trek to base camp for my "Everest Experience" because so many tourists did. I chose instead to head first toward other mountain giants that captivated me.

———————

Before the Prithvi Highway was completed eight years earlier, Pokhara, to the west of Kathmandu and second of the three cities in Nepal, was inaccessible by car or bus. People journeyed by mule or on foot, forced to cross several treacherous rivers thundering down from the peaks. The precarious bus that bounced me westward was itself a primitive means of transportation, but at least there was dirt "pavement" and modest bridges on my route. My guidebook suggested that Nepalese buses were held together by wire, string, and the collective hopes of everyone on board.

Pokhara was renowned for its stunning scenery because the high Himalaya rose so rapidly from its green plain. The mountains seemed to be leaning over the valley, close enough to touch. Dhaulagiri, Annapurna, and Manaslu, each a mammoth peak in its own right, dominated the northern horizon. Macchhapuchhare, the perfect pyramid peak, loomed above me. I had read about every mountain in the range, the Annapurna Range. As I gazed upward toward the blinding whiteness of those mountains backed by an indigo sky, I knew that I had to go there, to sit in the nave of such a precipitous cathedral.

An ancient place on the trade route between India and Tibet, Pokhara was the take-off point for expeditions and treks into those mountains. I heard that a British expedition from Hong Kong was commencing an ascent of the famed 23,000-foot Annapurna. I fantasized that I might be able to get on the mountain by offering to carry loads from base camp up to camp I. So, of course, I needed to discover the way to base camp.

I investigated the old part of Pokhara, streets lined with ancient brick Newari houses. Buffalo carts ambled down mud roads, and exotic peoples roamed the town, some with donkeys or yaks. The climbing fair, where expeditions consigned sherpas and local hill folk to guide and act as porters, was not hard to find.

A small, dark gentleman, speaking passable English with a British accent, stood on an elevated stage shouting instructions and calling out names. The area before him brimmed with people looking for work and a few climbers seeking staff for their expeditions. Approaching him, I explained I sought a porter whose extended family dwelled in the foothills. I'd hatched a travel plan: I wanted to carry my own weight along the trek and needed only one man from a hill tribe to accompany me. As small, swarthy men roamed the fields, I looked for a friendly little guy who might be my perfect companion on an impromptu trek. I wanted to hike all day and stay with the porter's relatives in their stick and mud huts at night, ultimately heading for Annapurna Base Camp. He knew just the person and called him up.

"Johnny" Tamang (the name denoting his tribe or clan) didn't speak a word of English. He was much shorter than my 5 '4". An unabashed smile with one missing tooth never left his face. His bright white teeth, dazzling in the Himalayan sunlight, contrasted with his dark skin. Johnny came attired with one layer of old clothing, no footwear, and a thatched basket that he carried on his back with a strap across his forehead to hold the basket in place. I had the manager explain to him that I would not let him carry my belongings; I wanted him there as my bridge to the inner lives of the Hill People. We took off an hour later.

We spent two glorious weeks trekking through the region, speaking our own personal sign language with infectious laughter. He seemed to find everything funny. That humor uplifted my already soaring spirits. Each night we shared in the hospitality of the mountain farmers we visited. They found it most amusing that Johnny was being paid the big bucks — a dollar a day — to hike around with an American woman and take her to their huts for meals and sleeping.

The Tamang people lived in miniscule one-room houses with a central fire and no ventilation in the roof. The ceilings were encrusted with soot, the air unpleasantly thick with smoke. No one seemed to notice although coughing was a constant affair. We sat around their cooking fires, eating the popcorn US mountaineers had taught the people to make.

An arduous, dizzying ascent left me breathless and exhausted as we climbed toward the Annapurna Range. The thin air made hiking challenging, but the marvel of the place with its vertical, glistening walls and its crashing, cascading river provided the impetus to keep putting one foot in front of the other.

Annapurna Base Camp sat regally at almost 14,000 feet, and was nothing like Everest Base Camp. There were no tents here — no garbage, no junk. A single shack made of rocks from the glacial moraine stood on the plateau. The male and female porters — barefoot, grimy, and grinning — who brought up the loads of gear and food for the Hong Kong expedition milled around in the cold. The climbers were nowhere in sight.

I looked around the peaceful sanctuary, smiled upon by the Hindu mountain gods, and wondered if it was irresponsible of me to imagine trying to get on the mountain by carrying loads while wearing sneakers, the only footgear I had. But in the face of such majesty, everything seemed possible. Perhaps, it was for the best that the opportunity did not present itself. Severe GI tract complications left me vomiting and dashing for my "outhouse" behind some large boulders during most of the 36 hours we remained there. Happily, before the malaise struck me down, I hiked far above the camp, to nearly 18,000 feet. There in the snow I found the gigantic, melted-out prints of a snow leopard.

Later in the journey, I crossed a bottomless gorge on a massive log with nothing to tether me to it or help me balance. Johnny went first, strolling as if on solid ground. I stared into the gorge at the foaming river, a turquoise white from glacial silt. As it raged far below, Johnny stood on the other side and gestured for me to come across. I knew not to look down, but the noise drove my attention to the abyss. I could not move. Johnny crossed back over to me and looked around on the ground until he found a long branch. He indicated that I should give him my backpack, which he hoisted on his own shoulders. He then gave a little demonstration of how, like a tightrope walker, I could balance with this rod. He handed the stick to me and breezed across the gap a second time.

If I hesitate another instant, I'll never make it across.

Johnny stood where I wished I was already standing and pointed to his eyes.

"Look at my eyes, not down," he was saying.

I trembled my way inch by inch across the chasm, using my stick as a psychological handrail. The only time during the trek Johnny did not smile his affable grin was while I crossed that ravine.

We spent part of one day on an ancient trail of steps carved into the stone on the side of a precipice. We passed what might well have been one of the last yak trains carrying salt from Mustang, Tibet, into Nepal, an ageless tradition. These were the real yaks, the ones who lived above 11,000 feet, all fuzzy and furry, creatures critical to the lifestyle of the Tibetans and Sherpa peoples.

Lonely Planet guidebook in hand, I made plans for my Everest encounter as the bus rattled back to Kathmandu. Since my lifestyle had evolved into seeking out the hardest, longest, and wildest challenges I could imagine, I was driven to find a way to create a personal relationship with the highest point on earth. Although I lived frugally on those excursions, I decided that I would chuck up the bucks to take a flight around Everest. A flight would, in a sense, allow me to both climb and summit Everest—with my eyes if not my legs. The guidebook also described a small hut in the foothills, easily accessible from Kathmandu, with a stunning view of the sunrise over Everest. Those two events struck me as the perfect alternative to hiking into Everest Base Camp.

On October 8th, I boarded a small plane to take me to the top of the world. The monsoon was ending. While there were heavy, billowy clouds sitting in the valley, the skies were a pristine blue. The day was clear, pure, and still. As the plane climbed above the clouds, the mountains grew larger by the second, glowing in their glacial glory. One famous peak after another came into view. Finally, the Mother Goddess beckoned, massive and beguiling, her head in space, her jet stream snow plume blasting into Tibet.

I was on the "view" side of the plane, beside myself with the thrill of this visual adventure. We couldn't really fly *around* the peak because the northern side was in Chinese air space and closed. But we spent a good hour in the air, being treated to the finest scenery in the world. The magnitude of the mountains challenged my perceptual reality.

I could see the summit out of my little, oval iced window as the Nepali pilot came on the loudspeaker: "Ladies and gentlemen. We are very happy to announce that today is a very special day. It is summit day for the American Everest Bicentennial Expedition. Two climbers are making their way to the top as I speak. I have radio contact with people on the mountain."

"Congratulations and good luck for a successful ascent, USA," he cheered with his British accent.

A garbled, scratchy response came from the mountain. I couldn't hear distinct words over the intercom system, but I felt that I was connected to that American team, that I was on the mountain with them. Experiencing their summit moment while looking down on the peak was better than climbing it — no danger, no frostbite, no risk of death — just the thrill and joy of their conquest. What incredible synchronicity — choosing that particular day in my life to fly to Everest.

I stopped at the information center to make inquiries about how to find the hut to watch the sun rise over Everest. Flirtatious black eyes with long eyelashes and a charming smile greeted me.

"Can I help you, Missie?" The male receptionist looked 14, but was probably my age, late twenties.

"Hi. I've been reading about this place in the foothills outside Kathmandu where you can watch the sun rise over Everest. I wondered about getting a bus that would drop me at the bottom of the hiking trail that leads there."

"Oh, yes, I know this place well. Many foreigners go there. But you don't need to worry about a bus. I have a motorcycle and would be happy to take you. If you come back at 4 p.m., I am finished with work."

Good English, cute smile.

I thought it would be fun to ride into the foothills with a young local. I pictured myself — hair blowing in the breeze, smelling the cool, clean air sifting down from the high peaks, arms wrapped around this handsome, friendly man.

Yet one concern nagged at me.

"Isn't four o'clock too late? I read that the climb's pretty long. I don't want to get there in the dark or get lost."

"Oh, no. This is a very easy hike. Two hours tops — just in time for sunset. You can't get lost."

I should have asked him if he had ever done the hike.

I watched the motor scooter, *not* motorcycle, disappear around a bend. I stood at the start of a well-worn but narrow dirt trail. All was silent. I didn't wear a watch, but the ride out clearly took much longer than I expected. We had puttered along at no more than 20 mph. It felt as if dusk was nearly upon me, and I hadn't even begun the hike. Clouds were building, obscuring the sun. I shouldered my backpack and hoped for the best. After all, this was the end of the monsoon season. I was strong and fit and knew I could make it to the hut much faster than the average tourist.

I looked upward at a trail that ascended quite steeply. That trail would take me from the subtropical valley floor to a ridge nearly 3,000 feet above. Nerves licked at the back of my mind like a wind about to turn into a tornado. The skies darkened more with each minute. A heaviness descended upon the land. The distinct smell of rain, steely and fresh, penetrated my nostrils. The monsoon was not over; the rain began. This rainfall was like no other I had experienced. It quickly became a solid, interminable sheet of water, a malevolent force. Within the hour, I was drenched, *and* it was pitch black.

The trail entered a bamboo forest, always climbing. The bamboo towered far above my head and gave me some shelter from the downpour. I said a little prayer of thanks for the protection. The guidebook hadn't mentioned what happened in bamboo forests during rainstorms.

As the trail rose beyond the bamboo wood through a pine forest, the rain blinded me, whipping my face with its icy tendrils. The temperature dove; my body temperature dropped in sync. The trail was slick with gummy earth, and my sneakers were sopping wet. I could feel the slimy mud slopping around inside my socks.

The track snaked up the hillside, becoming even steeper and very exposed to the elements. It funneled the precipitation, creating a forceful cascade down its middle. A cold, gummy fluid splattered my shins and knees. It was impossible to step off the trail into the brush and still walk, so I battled the water with every step and began to fear I wouldn't make it. I stumbled and slipped, clutching at woody vegetation to keep myself from being washed away. Hypothermia was seeping into my body: My teeth began to chatter, my muscles weakened with the increasing cold, my fingers and feet became numb. I had long since donned all the clothing I brought with me. I needed shelter. There was none. There was nothing but pelting rain, wind, and darkness. I felt so terribly alone.

A good three hours had passed when, from out of the blackness, a dim light bobbed off to my right, approaching quickly. A side trail connected to the route I was on, and someone approached. To my astonishment, a small man with a big umbrella suddenly stood before me.

"Wow, am I glad to see you," I gushed. "Do you speak English?"

He jabbered at me in Nepalese. I couldn't understand a word, but I guessed he was as surprised to see me as I was to see him. I'm sure that he wanted to know what the hell I was doing out there in the night in the monsoon. I might have asked him the same question.

Over and over I repeated the name of the tiny village where my safe haven awaited me. Clearly my pronunciation was not correct, yet eventually he caught on and started to repeat it himself. He gestured upward, then at himself. We were headed the same way. Because his flashlight was pointed at me, I could not see his features or his expression well, but I could tell that he was short and very muddy. I looked upon him as my savior. He knew where he was going; he had a light. If I collapsed he would be able to bring help.

My rescuer motioned for me to join him under the umbrella. It was awkward to trudge so steeply uphill in this river of mud under his shelter, but the protection from the downpour and the comfort of the presence of another human being were irresistible. I moved closer; our hips touched.

We struggled upwards, joined at the hip so to speak. Hail added to the mix of threatening elements. It seemed uncanny to be in physical contact with a strange man in a foreign country, fighting my way up a mountainside in the night's storm. I told myself that the Nepalese were a gentle people, that I was safe. I hadn't heard of women being assaulted in this country. Besides, how could a man think of attacking a woman in the middle of a monsoon downpour about to sweep both people away?

Then his arm reached around my waist.

He must realize how weak I am from the hypothermia. He must be trying to hold me up, help me keep going.

The rain blew sideways under the umbrella, almost ripping it out of his hand. He then reached up and cupped my breast.

He was not taller than me, but he was surely much stronger.

Could I run? I can't get away from him going uphill. If I head downhill I'll be stuck outside in the elements, weak and freezing.

His hands roamed as I struggled for an answer. I boiled with anger, livid with the thought that a man was taking liberties with me in such a dire situation.

I summoned up all my strength, making my face as aggressive and scary as a Tibetan oracle's mask and shouted:

"Take your goddamn ugly hands off of me, you monster. Take your fucking flashlight and umbrella and get away from me."

I shoved him with both hands and the full force of my body. The little guy was thrown backwards by my explosion, stumbling and falling into the brush. As he went down, the flashlight flew over his face. I surprised him; I *terrified* him!

A Nepalese woman would never act with such verbal and physical force. The guy lay sprawled in the bushes, shocked, and, it seemed, ashamed. He had probably tried to see what he could get away with, not intending to molest me and leave me for dead. I had sufficiently frightened him so that now he was the one who wanted to run.

He dragged himself up, head drooping in embarrassment, clothes torn from the shrubs and dripping with muck. He lifted the umbrella, which, fortunately, hadn't blown away and offered me its shelter once more. This time we made room between us.

The rain was a solid wall, obscuring the few lights of his village until we were upon it. He tugged on my wind jacket and pointed up the hill. He gestured to a tiny trail that ascended almost vertically. Our exhalations turned to ice fog; the rain turned to snow. He shuffled away toward his home, slumped in shame, as I bent low against the wind and dragged myself up the trail with the last of my strength.

No lights were visible, but I knew from the guidebook that the refuge was not far above the village. My soaked clothes became stiff as they began to freeze. I had to keep moving and pray that the guidebook was accurate. I didn't have much time left; soon I would drop, unable to go on. Then I would freeze to death.

The tiny, primitive hut appeared like an apparition in the storm. I couldn't feel my hands as I banged on the door, desperate for shelter. I could hear people laughing inside. The door opened.

The shack was dimly lit by an oil lamp, the glass tinged black with soot. Cots lined the walls; sleeping bags were spread out across the floor. Europeans and Australians filled the space. As I made my grand entrance, the laughter turned to silence. I realized that I arrived many hours after sunset, that I was so wet a puddle was forming on the floor around my shoes, and that I must have looked like a ghost because my face was surely a pallid gray from the hypothermia. But why was everyone aghast?

Something is very wrong.

I broke the spell by dropping my pack to the floor. Whispering began. I bent over, fumbled with the laces, and removed a sneaker, pouring out a good deal of watery mud. But even in the dim light I could see that it wasn't water. My shoe was full of blood. I tugged off the other one. It, too, was filled with blood. Everyone stared in horror.

I pulled off my socks. They were soaking with blood. My blue cotton pants were red. Blood dripped down my arms and off my fingertips; it trickled down my face. I stood in a pool of dirty crimson mud.

It was then I saw the little black creatures attached to my bare feet. They also clung to my hands and my face (and hid under my drenched clothing). A kind Australian fellow stood, walked up to me, and put a hand gently on my shoulder.

"Looks like you've run into an army of leeches, love."

"Leeches! These hundreds of tiny black streaks on my body are leeches? But I don't feel anything."

"You wouldn't, love. When they attach themselves, they inject an anesthetic which numbs your skin."

"How did I get them all over my body? How is this possible?"

"The bamboo; they live in the bamboo. You must have come through the forest after the monsoon began. The rain flushes them out of the trees. Nasty business."

"Why am I bleeding so much?" I cried.

"They inject a chemical called Heparin. It's an anticoagulant."

"How do I get them off? Can you help me get them off? Please. "

"Well, love, we need to burn them off, one by one. I will be happy to help you."

Someone made the charming comment that if they weren't removed each one could swell to the size of a ripe tomato.

"Did you know their suckers have three sets of jaws and hundreds of sharp, tiny teeth?" asked another helpful trekker.

I didn't know whether to throw up or faint.

Suddenly the group jumped into action. They offered me dry, warm clothing. Someone took my trashed shoes and put them outside the door. Someone else opened my pack, took out my pad and wet sleeping bag, and made a spot for me on the floor. A cup of warm tea was put into my frozen hands. Another lamp was lit to help with the procedure of removing the leeches. Everyone with matches contributed them to my cause.

As people crawled into their sleeping bags, the Australian, whose name I never learned and whose face I never really saw because I was so traumatized, went to work on my body. With the touch of a match, those damn, creepy creatures dropped off one by one until the floor was littered with them.

Sometimes I shook; sometimes tears ran silently down my face. Before the night was over, my body was free of leeches. My champion offered me his cot, which I gratefully took. I passed out in dreamless gratitude.

I had just fallen asleep when the group began stirring at 5 a.m. Light had yet to suggest itself upon that special day, but it would take time for everyone to dress, use the outhouse, and hike to the top of the hill before the first rays of the sun appeared. My body throbbed with fatigue, but the sunrise was one I was not about to miss. I donned the dry clothing people lent me and looked for my shoes.

"Anybody see a pair of bloody sneakers?"

"Yah, they're sitting outside the door on the porch."

I opened the front door to a blast of freezing air. The deck was covered in snow. My sneakers were solidly frozen and very gross. The monsoon had dumped six inches of watery snow that froze solid in the night. Under the snow, the ground was covered in a sheet of ice. If I wanted the experience, I was going to have to do the hike barefoot and without adequate clothing.

If people can walk barefoot over hot coals, I can walk over ice and snow.

We hiked solemnly in the pristine snow of a rosy dawn, taking turns breaking trail to the viewpoint, a tiny knoll rising in front of the greatest peaks on earth. We were a procession, there to worship Chomolungma. I absorbed the sunrise over the dazzling Himalaya, a religious experience of the greatest magnitude. The world glowed as the Mother Goddess smiled down upon me.

In 1986, the Annapurna Sanctuary was created, the first and largest conservation area in Nepal. The trek that I designed with Johnny is now offered by adventure travel companies and is billed as a "world-class adventure." There are internet cafés along the way.

Four airlines sell one-hour flyby tours of Everest these days. Their motto: "Conquer Everest in one fell swoop."

I learned years later that Arlene Blum, the most renowned female mountaineer of my generation, was part of the Bicentennial Everest Expedition. Her efforts to claim a place for women in the world of mountaineering have remained a life inspiration to me.

Chapter 7

VOLCANO

Bali, 1977

"I want to travel to the heart, to the precipice, to the depths, and
live it on its terms, understand it on its terms,
and then come back."

~ Warren Richey

The earth vibrates beneath my feet; the black velvet sky thunders, congested with clouds of ash. Genung Agung belches smoke and rock. The volcano is erupting with molten rage. Crimson red lava spews from the crater while massive, fast-moving currents of hot gas and rock travel away from the cataclysm in every direction.

As the rivers of destruction snake down the mountain, the people flee. People everywhere—eyes wild with fear—running, screaming, dying. No one will be spared. Not the peaceful Balinese, not me.

The gods are angry. They are angry with me. I'm bringing their wrath down upon this exotic island by climbing their high holy peak, their dwelling place. Me, a woman—sacrilege.

The island of Bali is vanishing in a nightmare of horror and destruction. The earth rocks so violently now that I must struggle to keep my balance.

Instead of flying into Bali's only airport with the tourists, I devised a land/sea route. I caught a train in Jakarta and traveled the slow, stop-and-go line across Java to the straits that separated Java from Bali. My third-class ticket allowed me to experience the flavor of poor Indonesia from an intimate perspective. Once we left Jakarta, villagers got on and off the train with chickens, goats, broods of children, and assorted luggage wrapped in rags. The ancient train rattled my hard wooden seat. I wondered if I would have blisters on my bottom before the trip ended.

The car was steamy, sweaty, smelly. A family entered from some nameless stop in the jungle. Seeing that the seat next to me was the only one left, they (a mother and two kids) slid into it. Curious children besieged me as I sat helplessly crammed against the window. Ragged clothing clung to their backs; flies circled their sweaty heads. A baby boy with big, brown eyes sat on the floor, pulling on my pant leg. Two girls climbed into my lap, giggling and patting my face with their tiny, sticky hands. From the seat behind me, someone tugged on my braid while an anorexic rooster pecked at my flip flop. What a party! Here was a microcosm of Javanese life. Bare feet, handsomely printed sarongs, hair decorated with jungle flowers put me in the center of loveliness. Kindness and mirth filtered through the muggy air.

The railway ended at the eastern tip of Java in a village with a ferry terminal where a dilapidated boat cozied up to a shaky dock. Those little ferries, always filled beyond capacity, plied the Indonesian seas and were notorious for sinking. We embarked. The play of currents, wind, and waves made the short crossing dangerous, but having grown up on the ocean in our fishing boat, I reveled in the wild ride as I recalled that joyous part of my childhood. The Indonesians on board huddled in family groups and either prayed loudly for a safe crossing or threw up over the side. I watched Java, a land of Islam and small volcanoes recede as Bali, an island of Hindu/Buddhism and a massive volcano, revealed itself.

An ancient bus awaited us on the Balinese side. I wondered how it could make it across the island to my destination, Denpassar, on its tread-bare tires. The seats were tattered, the metal flooring rusted. The windows stuck; some were cracked, some broken. The road across Bali followed the southern coastline, making for exquisite views of the Indian Ocean on my right and the volcano-dotted jungle on my left. Clouds shrouded the main volcano and hid its imposing size. Axle-pounding potholes cratered the dirt highway. I was surprised when the bus arrived at its destination intact only to realize that it made that trip twice a day, seven days a week. How I loved the Third World for its audacity, its tenacity.

In eleventh grade I dated a great guy, Denis, who was now a helicopter pilot for a British oil operation in Borneo. Denis had ex-patted to Australia and owned a vacation shack in Kuta Beach on Bali. He extended an open invitation for me to visit. How sweet can life get? My vision was to do something quite unlike me — lounge around and enjoy a taste of low-key living for a change.

"What are you doing here?" were the first words out of my mouth as I reached Denis's cottage. I expected him to be in Borneo.

Not only was he there; he wasn't alone. At his side stood a tall, sexy German *fraulein*. He'd met her in Sydney and invited her to Bali for a little love vacation. I guess I was disappointed but not crushed. He wasn't the great love of my life, and the letter announcing my visit wasn't exactly specific about my arrival date.

As a result, his response was: "What are *you* doing here?"

Denis was lost in lust and making the most of every minute of the night *and* day. I needed to look for a less embarrassing place to live, and what a great place I found. For about $1 a day, I rented a room in a Balinese compound, a rectangular affair with a shrine-flanked entrance. The interior of the compound consisted of a courtyard filled with chickens and many small buildings, including two shrines, the family sleeping quarters, and the kitchen. One of these structures — with a mattress of sorts on the floor and colorful fabric hanging over the door — was the *bale duah*, the guest pavilion. It became my new home for the next three months. The toilet/bath was a tiny building with a deep hole to squat above on one side and a water-filled bucket overhead on the other. The pull of a rope upturned the bucket, providing me with a shower. I needed nothing more.

All compounds were built with the same layout based on a design in accordance with *adat*, the traditional religious law of the island that dictated how peoples' homes were to be built — in which direction they were to face, the layout of each room in the compounds, how many temples they required, and their location.

The kind, extended family of that home cared for me and blessed my stay in that paradise. Their gentleness and laughter filled the space with a simple happiness I had never experienced. I sensed no stress there, no hurry in the way they moved about, prepared food or cleaned the compound, no worry about what tomorrow would bring.

Everything, every day, was a ceremony of joy. Each morning I found an offering of rice and dramatic tropical flowers at my doorstep, intended to keep away the evil spirits of the night. The island's unique variant of faith was a composite of Buddhism, Indian cosmology, and local animist traditions. Bali breathed the most deeply seated spirituality of any land I had yet visited. The Balinese lived with a consciousness of life's sanctity. Dwelling in this world was the beginning of a rich upwelling of inner growth for me.

With each new day, as I rose to the crowing of roosters and stepped through the beaded curtain of my doorway, my sense of gratitude for this kindness and care deepened. I wondered if I had ever felt more loved in my life. Though they spoke no English, the family's smiles and gestures communicated an unconditional embrace. I could not remember ever feeling such acceptance from my own family. Had I finally come home?

One of the most impressive cultural events on Bali occurred in the mountains during my stay, the two-day cremation ceremony of a member of the royal family. He must have been important—the last king, some said—for this celebration was an extravaganza of color, costumes, masks, parades, and music. The cremation occurred on day two. I saw bodies being burned from afar in India on the shores of the Ganges as I traveled downriver in a dugout canoe, but here I stood so close that I sweated from the heat of the fire, listening to the sizzling of the man's flesh. Singed hair, scorched skin, and boiling organs combined to create an acrid, sickening smell. Occasionally I saw fluid bubble out of the corpse and quickly evaporate. I was riveted to this macabre scene, choking on the smoke until nothing but hot ash and charcoal from the funeral pyre remained.

It would take me years to process the impact of this cremation on my spiritual development. I would think about how this deceased person was feeling no pain, no terror, no loss, while I was gripped in the horror of death and the threat of impermanence. I found myself quite relieved that they didn't burn the living widow with her husband as was the custom in some Hindu cultures at that time.

Looming over me during the cremation ceremony, nudging me, taunting me, was Genung Agung, Bali's greatest volcano. I was a mountain climber; mountains spoke to me and usually said: "Climb me." The peak was monstrous, rising directly from sea level to over 10,300 feet. It took up a goodly portion, perhaps a quarter, of the square footage of the island. It was frequently hooded in clouds, and its very presence created the island's weather.

Genung Agung was reputed to be the lofty home of the Balinese gods. The highest gods dwelled on the highest peak. Climbing a sacred peak any place on the planet is considered sacrilegious; it was no different here. My old, Catholic religion taught that God lived in a cathedral in a chalice, not on a mountaintop. While I could comprehend the sanctity for life of the Balinese, worshipping a volcano still eluded me. I did not wish to be a disrespectful foreigner, but I felt compelled to climb that mountain. My urge for adventure got the better of me. I couldn't take my eyes off the peak. I couldn't stop thinking about how to make a successful ascent.

Frustration followed my quest for climbing information; people came to Bali to lie on the beach, not thrash through the jungle and scramble up volcanoes. However I learned many facts: Agung was an active volcano. It last erupted in 1963-64 and spewed lava over its northeastern flanks. It generated massive pyroclastic flows—currents of gas moving down the volcano at speeds as great as 450 miles per hour with temperatures reaching 1,830 degrees Fahrenheit. Over 2,000 people were killed by the eruption.

The good news was there were no indicators that another event was imminent.

One day I dropped in to the only bar in Kuta, Fred's. An assortment of New Zealanders on holiday and the occasional Aussie could always be found drinking there. On that day Duke Duckett was downing a beer and chewing on a stinky cigar when I stuck my head into the little, darkened room. Duke had called Bali home for the past seven years. Since my arrival, I'd seen him around each day. Though he strode about in Hawaiian shirts and baggy shorts, intensity and alertness dominated his demeanor. I thought he was ex-CIA. The CIA-looking sunglasses he sported day and night might have had something to do with my impression.

I needed a cohort in this adventure and decided to approach Duke because he owned a vehicle. He was interested and offered to take me to the temple village of Besakih, the highest accessible point from which to approach the volcano. I needed to poke around up there. Who better to do that with than an ex-CIA agent?

The next day found us in his small Toyota pickup weaving through the populated centers and beyond into a hilly region of rice paddies. It was Spring. The terraced fields shone a brilliant jade and shimmered in the sunlight. Ever since, when hearing the word green, my mind has pictured that beautiful vision of terraced emerald landscape.

A zone of wild, tropical jungle lay above the paddies. Beyond that we entered a temperate jungle, dryer, cooler, with less luscious vegetation. The cloud-wrapped volcano towered above us. The ocean lay visible thousands of feet below, a sparkling, blinding turquoise.

The bumpy, single-lane dirt road ended abruptly at 3,600 feet above sea level at Besakih. Beyond the village not a single soul dwelled or traveled. While this was the official stopping point for all tourists, if I had my way, it would be my springboard into the unknown. From there my climb would ascend 6,288 feet, a daunting amount of uphill in any climate under any circumstances — well over a mile into the sky. Just how high, far, and hard would that be? I tried to imagine a ladder with as many wobbly rungs as the mountain was tall and tried to picture climbing it without using my hands.

The temple was actually a complex of buildings cascading down the hillside, the first stones dating back to megalithic times. Dwellings and simple tourist shops which all seemed closed bordered the dirt path leading to the temple complex. Besakih was the major pilgrimage site for the Balinese. That day quiet pervaded the town with neither Westerners nor pilgrims in sight. Dogs, chickens, and locals ambled about. Children played and several young boys hung out in the empty, dirt parking area. If I was going to find anyone to tell me about climbing the peak or, hopefully, someone to go with me, it had to be here. I hoped that one of those boys would be my accomplice.

I didn't need the words of Balinese I learned by studying regularly with the beach locals because the kids all knew some English, inspired to learn the rudiments by the mighty tourist dollar. The first three boys I approached gave me little hope.

"No lady. Nobody climb mountain. Not allowed. Bad, bad."

They impressed me with their seriousness, the tone of respect they conveyed. They believed the gods were up there on that peak. I wavered briefly as I thought that breaking their traditions might be too disrespectful a thing to do. But I rationalized that outsiders were constantly breaking time-honored religious dictates. More and more trespassers would come as the years passed. I locked my conscience in a tight little box in the back of my mind.

The fourth boy pointed out a fourteenish-looking youth leaning against a building and said:

"Ask him. He break many laws."

Wayan was my man. Short, dark, and indeed fourteen, he pranced about like the boisterous roosters at his feet. He exuded an air of confidence that attracted me. He looked fit enough for the undertaking.

Indeed, he was willing and seemingly eager to break the rules and attempt the climb. When I asked if he knew the way, he assured me he did. He'd never climbed the peak, so how could that be? Since he was my only candidate, I didn't ask and never did find out. Was there a whispered, oral tradition about the route that the villagers shared from generation to generation? Had someone he knew guided others and explained the way to him? In any case, I was going for it. I hoped to get lucky, a characteristic element in most of my high-risk adventures. When I asked about climbers before me, he replied that a long time ago a group of European men climbed the peak. I asked about women climbers:

"Lady not strong enough to try."

We'll see about that, kiddo.

I offered him a guiding fee of $10, an enormous sum of money in his world. He wanted $50; we settled on $20. If this kid could find the route as well as he could bargain, we would surely succeed. I instructed Wayan to be prepared with backpack, water, food, and clothing. The forecast looked hopeful for several days. Finally, I needed Duke's willingness in the transportation department. He agreed to drive me back in two days. Duke shook his head all the way down the mountain.

"That's a year's wage for a child, you'll ruin the economy," he laughed.

Maybe so, but the climb was on.

———————

I awoke, startled by a man calling my name in loud whispers. I looked up. The mountain was brooding in the moonlight. Duke was rocking the camper, trying to wake me without waking everyone in the village. I'd been sleeping on the roof. I looked down. Wayan stood next to Duke. It took but a moment to stuff my sleeping bag into its sack, put on my sneakers, and lower myself to the ground. My nightmare of the living-color, erupting volcano left me with more than a little trepidation. Silence pervaded the darkened village.

It was midnight. Was midnight a good time to begin? I didn't have a clue. I had no experience with jungles or volcanoes. I simply knew that I wanted to be back by nightfall the following day and that the endeavor was huge. Neither of us had a flashlight. We faded into the jungle, two black shadows floating through a moonscape night.

Walking in the dimness of this mysterious place, I quickly lost my sense of time. We reached a small, deserted temple. I couldn't say whether we had traveled 30 minutes or two hours. Wayan finally spoke:

"We must make offerings. The gods will be terrible mad."

He went to the shrine; I stayed back. He made a burnt offering and began to pray silently. A part of me wanted to pray too—but to whom? Catholic guilt nagged while my nightmare roared in the back of my mind. There in the darkness, caught between the modern world and an ancient belief system, I became afraid.

But another part of me quickly interceded:

What! The Balinese gods are going to be so outraged they're going to cause the volcano to erupt? Get real, Barbara.

After what seemed like an interminable length of time, Wayan finished his prayers, and we struck out into the night. The trek was easy at first, but the jungle unnerved me. I expected some kind of noise. Then I heard movement at my feet. I jumped back with a jerky start and a faint cry. Had a snake just crossed my path? I could see nothing.

The snap of a twig.

What dangerous animals roamed this jungle at night? I sensed a definite presence. Could it be the *samong*, the Balinese tiger, stalking me? In Fred's Bar I saw the last photo of such a tiger—shot by a Dutchmen in 1925. Those tigers were considered extinct by '33. I was told it was "unlikely" that any still survived, yet my imagination ran wild:

Unlikely? Is there a chance that just a few of these cats are still alive? Is one watching me with its luminous green eyes, licking its chops, about to pounce?

96

Until dawn I could not shake the feeling that we were being followed.

As first light filtered through the humid, tropical greenery, I looked ahead. Wayan wasn't carrying a backpack. The route had no water. He was wearing jeans, a baseball cap, and a T-shirt, which would hardly do for the high altitude cold. I was pissed; he hadn't followed through on my directives. I would have to share my supplies and clothing with him and hadn't brought enough for two. Having no climbing experience, he didn't know how critical hydrating was to climbing. We were both already sweating profusely. I didn't like it at all, but here we were and had to make do. I would take care of the kid; he would get us up the volcano.

Eventually we encountered exceedingly steep slopes in an open forest with tall grasses waving like a sea of green serpents. Each steep step required a mountaineering gait: step, stop, breathe; step, stop, breathe. The first time I slipped, I grabbed chunks of grass in both hands — and screamed. This was some sort of saw grass, each blade as sharp as a razor. I looked at my profusely bleeding palms. Not once had Wayan touched the grass. As I wiped the blood off on my shirt, I resented his not warning me.

Navigating those steep pitches was challenging, but we made good progress. The trees thinned and became stunted. In the pale dawn, six hours after our departure, I could finally see the volcano cone above tree line. It rose rugged and primal in a cerulean blue sky. The ridge we would have to reach to make our way to the crater was visible far above us.

The volcanic tuff was crumbly with no stability; every step upward meant a slide backward with nothing to hold onto. I reached my arms straight out and pressed against the rubble with my hands for balance. To make each movement safe, I kicked steps into the earth the way one does ascending high-angle snow.

We both struggled and panted with effort. I sank into a moment-by-moment movement meditation, just one sweating step after another hour after hour.

We took our first break at the ridgeline. The fin proved to be perilously narrow, so narrow that I straddled it to drink some water and down a snack. Wayan declined the food and water I tried to force on him.

I worried:

What if he has a crisis up here? I couldn't possibly carry him down. Could I ever find my way back alone to go for help?

Not once did it occur to me that something could happen to me, that I could be helplessly stranded at altitude, left to die. After years of wilderness adventure, I had not yet come to grips with my mortality (although the Balinese cremation got me working on that). I had not yet conditioned myself to accept the possibility of negative outcomes. Yet the history of my adventures reeked of close calls. What was I thinking? I wasn't.

Once on the ridge, we looked across the entire island. I saw nothing but tropical vegetation in myriad shades of green punctuated by over a dozen tiny volcanoes. For a moment I could imagine that I had escaped the modern world and was back in a time when tigers really did roam the jungle and life was pure and simple. Of course, in that world I would be wearing a sarong and herding a flock of beautiful, snotty-nosed babies.

Hey, I'd rather be climbing.

We gingerly started the ascent of the fin. Walking on a ridge like that was extremely laborious. It required perfect concentration and good intuition. A false step would send us tumbling down one side or the other to our deaths. More than once each of us took a step that didn't quite hold our weight. Rocks and scree rumbled down the slope, disappearing in ever more distant echoes. Surges of adrenaline zipped through my veins. If only I had climbing gear. But who traveled to Bali for a vacation on the beach with climbing gear in their luggage?

As we carefully continued upward, I thought I felt a vibration under foot. Then stillness returned. Had I imagined it? Again. This time Wayan felt it too. He turned to me, pallid, despite his dark skin tone. Then a vague, buried rumbling occurred. Was it Genung Agung or the whole island that was coming to life? Pebbles loosened from the dirt and skidded down the ridge. We looked up, expecting to see — what? — smoke pouring from the crater? But no, the sky was still a pure blue. A deep-in-the-earth sound growled in the thin air.

I felt the chemistry of fear in my body: dry mouth, lightheadedness, thumping heart, moistened palms, sewing-machine legs. We were totally vulnerable. We could not run; we couldn't even hold on.

"What is it?" I shouted.

"The gods," said an ashen Wayan. "The gods are speaking; the gods are not happy. We must go down."

While I stood pondering this impossible predicament, I heard a *poof*. Far in the distance a puffy, white cloud hung above one of the lesser volcanoes. It hadn't been there a second before. Then another *poof*. A second volcano belched a little smoke cloud. It reminded me of a smoker blowing smoke rings. It also reminded me of my nightmare.

"Have you ever seen this before, Wayan?"

Terror taunted him. He shook his head no, speechless.

I speculated that perhaps this was a common phenomenon on a small volcanic island with an active volcano. I wished I had talked to a volcanologist before this trip. I wished I *was* a volcanologist. Did I think that knowledge would overcome whatever nature had in store?

Yet, I sure as hell wasn't going to turn around now. Quitting was simply not in my nature. Besides, if something calamitous were about to happen, we wouldn't escape it. If the mountain blew, it would destroy everything on our end of the island. And so, while the earth trembled and hiccupped and those little volcanoes put on their smoke show, I negotiated with Wayan about continuing upward:

"Hey guy, remember our deal? You get paid if you don't quit before the top."

He said nothing but lagged behind me as I cautiously returned to climbing. We moved up the jagged ridge, two tiny, insignificant specks, while Bali belched, steamed, and shook. Near the top, the ridge melded with the mountain. Looking ahead I saw what looked like a cliff. I hoped it wasn't. But then there we were, separated from our goal by a short but steep, crumbling wall. There was no way around it. We were both wearing sneakers, not ideal footgear for rock climbing. Because I hadn't intended this adventure, I traveled with lightweight shoes. Because his only "shoes" were flip flops, Wayan had borrowed a pair of sorry-looking canvas tennies from a friend.

The climb looked doable. It didn't appear to be more than 25 or 30 feet high. The hand and footholds seemed more than adequate for a novice climber. But there were three problems: One, the "rock" was rotten rubble; two, it was vertical; three, the only thing Wayan had ever climbed was a palm tree.

A rope would have been nice.

I told Wayan to stay put and watch me. His eyes were large dark saucers of doubt. He looked up the wall and then down the thousands of feet he would fall if he lost his balance. He quivered uncontrollably. Then he seemed to sink into a trance of immobility. We were so near. This stupid, crumbly cliff could not keep me from the top. I considered deserting him to gain the top by myself. But leaving him there didn't seem right. His vulnerability begged me not to abandon him for the summit.

A pep talk popped out of my mouth. I appealed to his athleticism; I assured him that he would do fine. Then I realized I just needed to climb. I figured that a fourteen-year-old boy couldn't stand to have a woman show him up.

"Okay, Wayan, here I go. Remember; watch carefully so that you can put your hands and feet where I put mine. I promise you will not fall."

I moved up the pitch, which wasn't quite as easy as it looked. Each place I touched was loose with disintegrating rock. I carefully ascended and made sure not to rely on just one handhold in case it broke off. I used my balance to maintain my stability. With deep relief I finally gained the flat top. If I was scared, it was going to be really hard on the kid.

I dropped to my knees and plopped down on my belly looking over the edge with as much enthusiasm as I could muster.

"See Wayan. Easy!"

I reached down, extending my arm toward him, as if I could pull him up. He seemed very far away and very small. He put out a hand to steady himself as fright made him dizzy. He looked up at me with uncertain eyes. Then he began his first, painfully slow, rock climb. To say that I was worried would have been an understatement.

"That's good. Yes. Put your right hand up there. Keep breathing. Don't take such a big step; there's a foothold by your knee. Keep moving. Don't look down, Wayan. You're doing great. Just a few more feet."

"Way to go, kid." He lay on the ground catching his breath next to me, bug-eyed, chest heaving.

It was then that the concept of responsibility crashed down on me like a well-aimed coconut falling from a tall palm tree. I had put myself in harm's way more times than I could count. But today I brought another human being, a child, with me on a dangerous, uncertain undertaking. His life was in my hands, not the other way around. That realization shook me as much as the earth had when it went into spasms earlier in the climb. There was nothing to do but be grateful that we were both safe — be grateful and get down without incident.

As Wayan regained his color and his breathing steadied, we looked toward the caldera. Now I allowed myself the kind of excitement reserved for those moments when success is assured. All that remained was the straightforward walk to the crater's edge.

We hiked giddily like two astronauts on the moon, sucking in the thin atmosphere. A smell of rotten eggs hung in the lean air. A lightheaded joy bounced back and forth between us. The baby volcanoes had stopped puffing smoke. The mother volcano stood solidly still under our feet. An old, vague trail followed along the crater's edge. Indeed, others had been there, probably approaching from the other side of the island. I was disappointed, but consoled myself that they hadn't come via *our* route, and that they hadn't come recently.

We stared into the caldron. It was large, deep, and foul, bubbling with noxious gas. I peered into the bowels of the earth. The mountain was dramatically alive. Looking east, I could see Rinjani, the highest volcano on the neighboring island of Lombok. The sea was lost in a salty haze; fair-weather clouds dotted an opaline sky. A cold breeze raised goose bumps on my arms. We wedged the white flag I had made from a stick and an old, white pillowcase among the rocks. With my cardboard, throw-away Kodak camera, Wayan snapped a photo of me. I took one of him with the many small volcanoes in the background. Was that pride etched on his face — or humility? The loftiness, the massiveness of this giant of the Indonesian Archipelago, stunned us both into awe and silence.

Just once in my life I wanted to be the first woman to stand atop an imposing mountain. I prevailed that day. My strength

and my will brought me there. I was on top of the world —
Wayan's world.

You can find a detailed description of how to climb
Genung Agung on the Internet these days. Many people
have climbed this peak in recent decades, but mostly
from the northern side.

The southwestern route (our route) is categorized as
"quite tough," although now there is a trail to follow.
The recommendation is to do a two-day ascent making
camp about two-thirds of the way up on day one, then
finishing the climb and descending on day two. We
made it up and down in 20 grueling hours. You can hire
guides with experience who will take you to the top but
not stand on the summit in deference to the gods.
Perhaps Wayan's grandson is one of those guides.

Ice Axe

My first day on rock. The Shawangunks, 1968.

Ice Axe

While we looked like hippies, we were serious athletes.

The faux summit shot after our ascent of the Grand, 1970.

High
Sierra

With friends in Yosemite Valley before
my backcountry adventure, 1971.

Despite my High Sierra debacle, cross
country skiing became a way of life.

I skied into the "Women's Elite" at
the Engadine Ski Marathon, ahead
of 26,000 racers

Musher

Shadows of Earl and I
training on the VW
chassis, late autumn.

The red eskimo
parka I sewed.
It's forty below.

Musher

Harnessing a team at Howling Dog Farm,
Autumn, 1972.

Nat and Race Marshal
Dick Tozier, at the
Anchorage track
before the race.

After the race.
Bad dog, Peggy!

Musher
How she got 'hitched'

By ALLAN FRANK
Daily News Staff Writer

Barbara Belmont only finished fifth in the Women's World Championship Sled Dog Race, but she figures that she was a winner anyway.

For a cheechako from North Babylon, N.Y., who never has owned a dog, and has mushed for only 5¼ months, Miss Belmont did well against the top female mushers in the country.

Using a team borrowed from Earl Norris, she ran sixth the first heat and fourth for the second and third heats. Her steady hand, "geeing" and "hawing" made her the fourth highest money winner with $135, a'though veteran musher Sue Hoiscław nosed her for fourth in the total time by 2 minutes, 23 seconds.

Miss Belmont got hitched to dog racing almost by accident. Her wanderlust brought her to Alaska with a mountain-climbing expedition last May. One member of the expedition knew Earl Norris, so they waited two weeks at his Willow homestead for the weather to clear on the east face of Mt. Huntington.

While they were waiting, Norris unspooled some of his home movies of dog racing and Miss Belmont was hooked. The expedition team which had given her a ride here from the Lower 48 didn't have room to take her on the mountain, so after their ascent she went back to New York to map her return to Alaska as a dog-keeper and general hand at Norris' Howling Dog Farm.

Every morning, she puts on her homemade mukluks, moose leather mittens and parka to make an hour and a half trudge with a shovel and an akio (sled) in hand. In exchange for room and board, she cleans, waters and exercises most of Norris' 90 dogs.

Before the weather got really cold, her routine started at 6:30 a.m. with a stint of reading, cross-country ski touring, puppy feeding and dog house cleaning. After lunch, she exercises "from one to five dog teams" on eight mile runs, then helps with dinner and rests.

"Now that it's really cold, I get up about 9 a.m., sit around and have a cup of coffee . . . When the days were short, there just wasn't any point in getting up any earlier . . . I feed and clean water a lot," Miss Belmont says.

Her enjoyment of mushing is moderated only by the temperature. "I was out one night driving in the dark and it was below 50 below. It's not fun when it gets that cold," she says. "The dogs don't seem to mind."

She's suffered several black eyes from running into trees with wild dog teams, but never has been bitten or

Musher Barbara Belmont

frightened by one of the Siberian huskies. "I'm very close to the dogs. I spend a lot of time with the dogs. After the days that I've raced this weekend, I go out and give them all little rubdowns to make them feel good. You do it just the way you give a person a rubdown."

Most of her 10 dog team are animals Norris and his son, J. P., are prepping for their first string of racers for the Men's Rondy race next year. "I don't have any specific dogs. Earl's given me different dogs to try out. I

don't drive the first string and I don't have my own team," she says.

Mushing has made her muscular, she says. At 5 feet, 4 inches, and 120 pounds, she can hold a 10 dog team. "I know I can. I've been passed a lot . . . I like racing for the sensation of speed; I like training for the sense of being alone in the woods," she says.

Next summer, she figures things will just as adventurous. Miss Belmont, the landlubber, wants to sign on with a crew in a small boat and sail around the world.

Made the front page! Anchorage Daily News, 1973.

Wanderings in Nepal

Heading into the Annapurna Sactuary.

Above base camp.
Annapurna in the
background.

Volcano

Denis and I on Kuta Beach.

My Balinese family at the compound.

On the summit of Genug Agung, 1976.
The cauldron is on my right.

Volcano

Wayan facing north. The small volcanos in
the distance were acting up during our ascent.

Billy Hayes and I,
sophmore year, 1962.

Prisons

Reunited. Christmas, 1975.

Prisons

With Helga and Hans on the Black Sea
Freighter, 1976.

On the road to Iran. Mount
Ararat in the background.

Heidi

In summer I took to the high peaks, 1978.

Ski mountaineering. At the edge of a massive crevasse.

Grizzly

Downriver Dick on the
way to Jackson Lake.

Bobbe kayaking on Jackson Lake
with the Tetons in the background.

116

Seeking the Sacred Jaguar

The view from my deck with Chuck's sailboat and the Caribbean in the background.

Mosquito coils were an essential part of life.

My beloved Tootsie.

*Seeking
the
Sacred
Jaguar*

I felt more at home underwater than on land.

Life on the atoll. I donned a
bikini for the photo.

Hauling in a BIG
barracuda.

Chapter 8

PRISONS

Iran, 1977

"Within yourself deliverance must be searched for, because each man makes his own prison."
~ *Edwin Arnold*

The fledgling CIA pulled off its first covert operation in Iran in 1953, returning Mohammad Rez Shah Pahlavi, the Shah of Iran, to autocratic rule as its puppet. The Shah, fearful of his political opponents, created an intelligence agency trained by the CIA that became notorious for its violence and brutality. A CIA Iran analyst said that in the late 70's the CIA taught these fiends Nazi torture techniques.

In addition to the standard devices, it was known to use such tactics as nail extraction; snakes; electrical shocks with cattle prods, frequently into the rectum or vagina; cigarette burns; sitting victims on hot grills; dripping acid into nostrils; water boarding; mock executions; inserting broken glass and pouring boiling water into the rectum. Considered the most hated and dreaded organization of the regime because of its penchant for torture and murder, its tactics brought terror to the hearts of Iranians. Its name was SAVAK.

I took the trip because I had been betrayed, because my heart was broken, because I believed no one cared whether I lived or died. The proclivity to punish myself for the hurtfulness of others tunneled outward from my subconscious like an alien creature erupting from a hidden cave. In an unspoken, subliminal sense, the journey was intended as a suicide mission to Turkey.

In September, 1975, my childhood friend, Billy, and I were reunited after he pulled off a recklessly brave jailbreak from a Turkish prison in the Aegean Sea. He escaped five years into a life sentence for smuggling hashish. He was my first love, though certainly not my only love. The years of his incarceration led me to believe he was my ultimate love. I returned to New York to be with him, imagining that dreams did come true, that we would spend our lives together, happily.

But when he stepped off the plane in New York, swarmed by media, an instant icon in a culture obsessed with drugs, I seemed to vanish from his radar. We moved into an apartment in Manhattan where I languished for a few lonely months while he worked on a book, delighted the media with his boisterous personality, and was wooed by Hollywood with the prospect of a world-class film about him, drugs, and imprisonment abroad.

After those months of painful exclusion from his life and fame, I left behind my shattered dreams and returned to Switzerland, where I'd been living before he escaped. I received a letter a month later, confessing that he had been screwing around with many other women, that he would only ruin my life, that I should forget I'd ever known him. A bizarre urge arose in me to end my life where he had almost lost his. I boarded the Orient Express in Vienna and headed for Istanbul.

Billy's escape made the front pages of the Istanbul newspaper; in the upper right hand corner, a sketch of me, his purported accomplice, glared at the Turkish readership. They had it wrong; I wasn't his collaborator. But I was his girl and the number one person on his contact list. I visited him; they saw my face. He left my pictures and letters behind when he fled.

In my despair, my thoughts ran something like this:

When I cross the border into Turkey, some official will recognize my name. I will be imprisoned as Billy's co-conspirator and rot away in the Turkish prison from which he escaped, leaving me a prisoner of betrayal and heartbreak.

No leap off a bridge for this defiled heroine. My demise had to be as dramatic as his deception.

But the Turkish authorities weren't on their toes. As the fabled Orient Express crossed the border, no one detected the infamous American criminal, Barbara Belmont. My death wish wouldn't allow me to walk up to police headquarters and turn myself over: I had to be caught. I was a very confused young woman who, in a whirlpool of heartbreak, became quite gifted at making up high-drama scenarios.

I arrived in Istanbul where I had visited Billy in prison during his incarceration. I roamed the crowded streets, finding the cheap room surrounded by spires and glittering golden domes where I last stayed. I wondered what came next. Hanging out in a coffee house one day as loudspeakers scratchily announced the call to prayers, I discovered that I could catch a freighter that traveled the Black Sea from Istanbul to the border of the USSR, stopping at ports along the way. I figured that since I had sentenced myself to entrapment in Turkey, I might as well tour around a bit rather than sit there, bored, brooding, and waiting for...what?

Belching ships chugged back and forth from Europe to Asia on choppy waves flecked with polluted sunshine. The powerful currents of the Bosporus Straits shifted turbulently from north to south and heaved at the hull of the boat. I stood on deck, loving the feel of the sea under my feet and the sounds of freighter horns echoing between continents. A couple stood at the railing, watching Istanbul evaporate in the distance. She was tall, hefty, and full-bosomed with long, stringy brown hair. He was short, thin, and looking a little hen-pecked. Helga and Hans Schmidt were on vacation, repeating a journey they had taken every summer for years.

I introduced myself in German and then asked:

"Where are you heading?"

"Isfahan. The tanker carries our station wagon. We camp along the route," Helga replied back in English.

What serendipity. I had run into fellow adventurers.

"And you? Where is your husband?"

"I am traveling alone," I explained.

"Such travel is far too dangerous for a woman without a man. You *must* come with us." That was Helga's assertive German nature speaking.

I explained I could take care of myself and thanked them for their gracious concern. Despite my declaration of self-sufficiency, Helga became very protective of me.

I relished the journey, the old ports, travel through an ancient world. The days of floating on the sea grounded me. Because I'd grown up on the ocean, I always came back to myself in, on or around water. In fact, as the smells of the water, the sounds of the gulls, and the rocking of the boat calmed me, I deeply questioned if I really was distraught enough to destroy myself. But there I was, trapped within the borders of a prison I had personally created, first within my psyche, then within Turkey.

At the end of my sea journey, a third-world bus transported me to Erzurum on a full-moon night through a vast, barren moonscape. There were other women on the bus. They were covered from head to toe in the chador, sitting in the back, like Blacks in the old South, silent, invisible. I too sat in the back feeling terribly conspicuous, unsafe, and lost.

Will coming to Turkey prove to be the worst decision of all the poor decisions I have made in my life? I asked myself as the moon shadows kept me company through that sleepless night.

The bus arrived late in the morning to changed weather, a dismal downpour. Erzurum was the only major city on the high plains of eastern Turkey. My five-dollar-a-day guide led me to the cheapest part of town, filled with seedy buildings and streets indented with potholes the size of big, black kettles. A miserable blanket of cold, gray clouds covered the ghetto. I thought I was seeing the real Erzurum, unaware of the city's illustrious history, housing empires over millennia. Its strategic location made it a fortress site that all the great conquerors coveted. It had been NATO's southeastern-most airbase throughout the Cold War. I was oblivious of that fact as well.

I found lodging in a shoddy hotel. Trudging up the rickety stairs I heard a kind of music from the upper floor — the rain was pouring in through the holes in the ceiling of my room. Buckets and bowls caught the flow and resonated with the song of the water drops. Too demoralized to sit with the drips, I slipped out to find food. Turning a corner, I ran right into my sweet German friends. As we shared a meal of rice and lamb, Helga again tried to convince me to join them. Their car was brimming over with camping gear and German foods. I had no idea where I would fit.

My travels finally brought me to my senses. I realized the only person I was punishing was myself. Billy probably wouldn't care if I vanished forever. I wanted to survive and had to escape Turkey safely. I decided to take the bus to Iran, which seemed a much safer place. I'd heard something about a major American military presence there. Even though I was traveling around the world, I paid little attention to international politics.

What do politics have to do with me?

Snow blown mountains flanked the road as my bus voyaged through what seemed a high-altitude wind tunnel. I was on a highway to nowhere with nothing to be seen but a ribbon of rutted black pavement and a barren plain. A place where the temperature could drop to 40 below in winter qualified to be called desolate. As the bus left Dobuhayazit, the only other place on the route to the border, my anxiety increased like a balloon being filled with air—a black balloon. I dared not think about what barbaric treatment I would receive if the Turks discovered me at the border crossing.

How could I have done this to myself?

As we drew closer, massive, snow-covered Mt. Ararat, purported home to Noah's Ark, towered to the north. Finally, in the east, the remote border crossing appeared, a ramshackle building in a god-forsaken land, no matter what the Bible said.

The sun dipped below the ragged, rocky horizon. I followed the other passengers, mostly Iranian men, into Turkish customs, backpack in tow. Would I be identified at the moment I was about to rectify my madness?

A small, dark man in a dirty, crumpled uniform instructed us to place our luggage on a pile. The guards looked through it casually and moved it to the bus, parked on the Iranian side. The Iranian bus driver reloaded the bags and boxes. Had I been able to stand and watch, I would have seen that my backpack remained behind.

As we stepped through the doorway into a clean, well-lit room, the soldier at the door took our passports. With an air of indifference and boredom, men sought out seats to await the return of their identity papers.

I was across the border, which meant I was safe. The Turks didn't even do a check on people exiting the country. My pounding heart eased as a breath of deliverance escaped my throat.

I took a seat in a white, oblong room with floors of marble and walls of another kind of white, polished stone. There were no windows. A large portrait of the Shah of Iran predominated the space. Wood benches lined the walls. My eyes drifted down a long hallway like two beacons searching in the dark. In an office at the end of the hall, I saw a rigid military officer at a large desk reviewing our passports. An ominous vibe rebounded back at me. Two guards, carrying rifles, flanked his door. As each passport was approved, he handed it to a guard, who walked the length of the hallway to our waiting room, called out a name, and returned the passport. The traveler was then free to exit and get back on the bus. The bus had been pretty full; it was a long process. As the outside door opened and closed, I could see that night was upon us. An ocean of stars twinkled in a sky where no lights obscured their cold beauty. My confidence thinned as the room became more and more empty. I felt a compelling urgency to have my name called.

Looks like I might be the last person back on the bus.

The final bus passenger left the building. It wasn't me. I heard the bus start up. It pulled away. Silence blared as the room morphed from a waiting room into a white sarcophagus.

I looked down the hallway to see the commander holding a passport, *my* passport. His eyebrows knitted, his mouth made words I could not hear as he read my information into an old, black phone. I stepped outside my body and willed it to flee with me. But my body sat frozen, immobilized by dread.

The tremors began. My flight or fight response hit hard. I shook so violently, I thought I might fall off the chair; I thought I might soil myself.

The officer put the receiver back on its cradle and called to the soldiers. Six pairs of army boots clicked across the marble corridor. Clack, clack, clack — like bullets hitting tin. The soldiers raised their rifles. One cold barrel pointed at my skull, another at my heart.

The officer said: "Belmont Barbara?"

I mouthed one of the most difficult words I had ever spoken: "Yes."

"You wait."

That was all he said. He turned, marched back to his office and picked up the phone, again looking at my passport. The faces of my guards were frozen as hard as the steel of their rifles.

'You wait'? If they're returning me to the Turks, why don't they just march me the few feet back to the Turkish side?

I wished I were out there in the icy night. I would run and run and run.

The man in charge was headed toward me again as two other men entered from the Iranian night. I thought, just perhaps, that I had begun to hallucinate. The new players were clearly Iranian, yet they looked like cartoon images of CIA agents: beige trench coats, spit-shined black shoes, black sunglasses (even though it was pitch dark outside), holstered guns beneath their jackets. This was no cartoon.

The officer handed them my passport, shouting out instructions to the soldiers. I was poked to my feet by the rifles and marched outside behind the sinister agents. I stumbled down several stairs to find a black car with windows tinted black sitting at the curb. A frigid wind blew; my spirit was already chilled to the freezing point. One of the men pushed me into the back seat. He sat beside me, his gun purposefully visible. A thump in the trunk suggested that my backpack toppled in. We sped off into the darkness.

As terrifying as those hours were, I guess I was lucky that I was apolitical. Had I known more, I would have realized that I was in the custody of two SAVAK agents. Savage SAVAK, the Shah's "intelligence agency," his personal death squad.

The road was bereft of any signs of life. Only the bouncing headlights and the stars offered direction. The driver negotiated the highway excessively fast; not a word was uttered. I was a captive. Men in black glasses with guns were taking me into a strange country without an explanation. I lost track of time and sank into a lifeless daze of fear.

It was close to midnight when I saw lights in the distance. We pulled off the highway into a sleeping town. A dusty road ran through the village. The buildings were all one story, made of clay bricks, the same hue as the desert.

The car stopped at what appeared to be an ancient fortress. 12-foot high walls topped with spiraling barbed wire surrounded a massive compound. The streets sat empty but for guards who stood on either side of two swinging doors made of large planks of wood, the entrance to the installation.

I peered through those doors into a military complex with big buildings and low-slung shacks. My SAVAK captors vanished with the car. I was prodded into the enclosure by a silent soldier. I kicked up puffs of desiccated earth as I walked across the yard, a rifle jammed firmly into my back. The jabbing firearm dictated my direction. An inky blackness leaked from the door he pushed me toward.

They're bringing me here to kill me. Will there be many soldiers? Will they rape me first?

In the middle of that night, only the mute world listened to the sound of my feet shuffling across the dirt. I felt faint, disoriented; the many hours without fluid or food and the desert's dust left my body dissipated. My heart pounded in my head. A terror too immense to consider shadowed me as I moved closer to the door.

The guard yelled something at me in Farsi, pushing me hard with the rifle toward ancient, clay stairs that descended into gloom. The steps were hard to maneuver until I discovered a wall to my left. I reached out for balance, feeling rough, dry mud and tried not to fall down into the blackness.

I must be dreaming.

This was like a scene out of a movie, out of Billy's movie. I was in a large basement. It was empty but for a beat-up table near the opposite wall and two metal folding chairs, one behind the desk and one in front. On the desk was a large, blinding spotlight pointing at my chair. The light faded toward the corners of the room, leaving the walls invisible. I imagined them crawling with hairy, black tarantulas.

Behind the light sat an Iranian in what looked like American clothes, his shirtsleeves rolled up, a cigarette dangling from the side of his mouth. On the desk sat my passport and a revolver.

"Sit," demanded my inquisitor.

"Your name is Belmont Barbara?"

"My name is Barbara Belmont."

"No, your name is Belmont Barbara. I have here your passport."

The light was painful; I turned my head.

"You look at me."

I shifted my head back in the direction of his voice and began to answer a series of questions that he repeated *ad nauseum*: Where was I from? Why was I coming to Iran? Why had I entered Iran by such a remote border crossing? What were my political views? What did I think of the great Shah?

Hours passed. The chair became painfully hard and cold, the spotlight, maddening. My lips cracked; my throat parched. A sinking fatigue made it hard to stay focused or respond. The agent who grilled me was becoming more and more annoyed, a dangerous annoyance. But I had no other answers for him. I knew nothing about the politics of his country or its leader; I cared less.

How many hours has he been interrogating me? Six?

Total exhaustion consumed me. I wanted him to stop, but I didn't want him to stop. Yet the moment came; he finished. He shouted something. A soldier ran down the stairs, approached my chair, and shoved his rifle into my back. I instinctively stood on weakened knees. Perhaps this was the worst moment of the entire ordeal.

Now. Oh my God. Now they're going to rape and kill me.

Brutal shoves from the rifle propelled me up the stairs. As we left the cellar, I was aware that the first light of dawn was seeping sadly in a delicate pink hue from the darkness.

The last light I'll ever see.

The soldier pushed me forward using a brusque gesture with his gun. Then my mind blanked out.

I found myself standing at the fort's entrance.

How is it I am standing at the gate?

I had crossed the compound in a trance. The soldier shouted at me, probably saying something like:

"Get out of here, you stupid whore, before we take you back."

I stood staring through the open entrance at freedom, unable to move. A thud to my back jettisoned me over the threshold.

Standing just outside the gate, still in shock, I looked down into the eyes of a Tibetan Mastiff-looking dog, a monster guard hound being held on a thick, rusty chain by one of the sentries. I made eye contact with the beast—a grave mistake. The dog lunged at my calf and clamped down. His huge mouth fit around my lower leg. My immobile state probably saved that leg. Had I tried to pull away, he would have torn my calf to shreds.

Instead, I stood as still as stone, disbelieving that a dog attack was the final punctuation mark on the experience. The guard lifted the end of the heavy chain that held the animal and pounded the dog over the head repeatedly. It let go, and I haltingly stepped away. My leg ached badly and bled from multiple teeth wounds.

"Barbara, Barbara."

Is someone calling my name? Surely I've lost my mind.

Two people jumped from a dusty VW station wagon, waving furiously for me to come toward them, away from the dog, the soldiers, the prison. My guardian angels, Helga and Hans, were there! I limped in their direction as they ran up to help me. They embraced me and quickly walked me to the car. I tried to speak but could not.

A few minutes later we pulled into a primitive, motel-like lodging where they had found a room. Hans started pouring me shots of schnapps.

"You need to relax; you need to sleep. Take my medicine. You are safe now," he said lovingly.

I slept until 3 p.m.

Hans and Helga had followed the bus to the border. Their vehicle was checked and waved through. They parked on the Iranian side and watched as the bus filled and pulled away without me. They then sat, waiting, for what they thought was about an hour. They saw the black sedan with tinted windows pull up. They observed the SAVAK agents enter the building and exit with me in tow at gunpoint. They then did the most unimaginable thing: They followed us with headlights off. They said that between the bright stars and the lights from the SAVAK vehicle they had no trouble seeing the highway.

They watched me escorted at gunpoint into the prison and decided to take turns waiting to see if I came out. If I hadn't appeared by 8 a.m., they would drive to the U. S. Consulate in Tabriz and alert the authorities.

When I awoke we decided to leave immediately for Tabriz despite my traumatized condition. To our grave distress, the consulate was deserted—some sort of golf tournament was in full swing. The receptionist told us we would have to go to the embassy in Tehran.

The American bureaucrat slouched behind his broad desk at the Embassy, his big belly bulging over his belt, and laughed when I told him my story. My life had been in jeopardy, and he *laughed*.

"You're not the first woman we've had in here with a story like this," he said with disinterest. I wanted to strangle him.

"You've heard this story before?" I croaked.

"Yup, we keep trying to teach these guys—'these guys' being SAVAK—that in the US your family name is your second name. They just can't seem to *comprende*. They got a tip that a terrorist would be crossing the Turkish border to assassinate the Shah. The terrorist is supposedly female and her first name is Barbara. You are the third Barbara we have had in here."

"So what are you doing about it?"

"Nothin'," he drawled in what I suspected was a Texas accent. He tossed my passport across the desk.

"Nothing? Can't you lodge a complaint? How will you protect me? What will happen when I try to leave? What if I get rabies from the dog attack? What about other women with my name who try to cross the border?"

"Not our problem. You know, you don't want to mess with SAVAK. They do what they want. We can't do anything, but you could go to their offices and talk to someone there about getting clearance to leave the country without trouble."

"But I am an American citizen. You can't just send me out of here with no security."

"Sorry, lady. Next."

I located the address I had been given in a part of the city that no foreigners frequented. There was a line out the door. I waited two hours to get inside, then waited another hour. I sat in a huge room crammed with people. Their faces bespoke terror; I could *feel* the fear in the room. The putrid smell of stress sweat permeated the air; downcast eyes showed no light. The only sound was the conversation behind a closed door where a SAVAK official was dealing with supplicants looking for missing family members or hoping to leave the country. I was the only Westerner and the only woman.

By the time my name was called—Belmont Barbara, of course—I realized that never before in my life had I been in such a dangerous place as Iran. I knew from the depth of the palpable dread that some of the people I saw that day would disappear and that those whom they sought were imprisoned or dead. I was learning about politics very quickly. I wanted to flee, but I wanted a guarantee of safety more.

My indignation raged, but it would have been a mistake to be aggressive. I explained the story of my incarceration as the agent examined my passport. He seemed to find me surly, disrespectful.

"I have no interest in this. Leave."

Helga waved until their car was out of sight, headed back to Germany. We were both crying. These two strangers had risked their lives to save mine. Their kindness and daring not only rescued me that sultry dawn in front of the fort, but also freed me from the prison in my mind where I believed that no one cared whether I lived or died.

After their departure, I took a bus to a resort on the Caspian Sea where I met a young, educated Iranian engineer. Walking on the beach out of the earshot of the authorities, he told me the true story of the Iranian people, the Shah, the CIA, SAVAK. A certain innocence, with which I had lived my life, was stripped away. I had learned the meaning of repression.

I left the country without incident, traveling eastward into Afghanistan. I visited Iran just months before the death of Ayatollah Khomeini's son, when demonstrations first erupted and the Iranian world began to change. Before the Shah was ousted and the reign of terror came to its end, SAVAK had killed thousands and tortured countless people. I was lucky not to have been more brutally victimized.

We are each other's angels. Two strangers had stepped in and saved me. I hoped one day to be able to have my turn at rescuing another's life.

Chapter 9

HEIDI

Switzerland, 1978

"Love, Mercy, and Grace, sisters all, attend your wounds of silence and hope."

~ *Aberjhani*

I knew the Swiss Alps in their pristine splendor could be deadly in high summer. I knew that out of a flawless, alpine sky, storms could descend in solid blankets of wet, sticky snow, obscuring all visibility, killing climbers high on glacial massifs. Even a seemingly harmless hike in such a summer storm could turn into a life-threatening event.

I knew — and yet I went.

The Alps, young mountains with dramatically serrated peaks, etched a snowy backbone across central Europe. Wild glaciers cascaded between summits; turquoise ribs of snow separated crags with tumultuous compacted blocks of ice. Crevasses, ice falls, and bridges filled those peaks with beauty and menace.

That world was my home. In winter I stuck to the ski resorts (with considerable out-of-bounds adventuring) and to cross-country skiing. In summer I took to the high peaks. Traversing the Alps was my favorite endeavor. I slept in Swiss Alpine Club huts, skied over the glaciers and climbed mountains along the way. The classic route across the Alps was called the Haute Route, but there was not just one. Many such traverses crisscrossed France and Switzerland; I did them all. I carried a backpack with an ice axe, crampons, a rope, and clothing for extreme weather conditions. To climb, I stuck synthetic "skins," which prevented sliding backwards, to the bottoms of my skis. Descending a highly crevassed glacier tongue required threading my way between crevices, sometimes roped to my partner. The sun left me with a dark tan. People said my white, toothy grin was almost as dazzling as the glaciers on those stunning summer days.

My two friends, Heidi and Ursi, were spending their annual summer vacation hiking in the high alpine meadows while their husbands volunteered in a youth mountaineering program housed in army barracks atop a remote pass. The girls invited me to join them for a few days. That trip into the mountains was different—far less dangerous than my norm. Although I continued to prefer the company of men, it was a big deal to be invited to join other women in the out-of-doors. Lack of female companionship was a story I told for decades. While hiking didn't offer the sort of addictive thrill I thrived on, I knew how beautiful the meadows would be in peak bloom, knew how happy I would be traipsing through flowers up to my waist.

So I jumped into my VW bug, speeding up narrow, winding roads, zooming around scores of hairpin turns, breezes from the open window blowing my hair around like waving prayer flags. The scent of melting snow on the air and a John Denver tune on the wind accompanied me on my journey. I sang at the top of my lungs until I stepped out of the car at the barracks three hours later.

———————

I awoke the next morning to a major surprise: A mid-summer snowstorm blotted out the blue skies that ushered me into the Alps just the day before. The snow was warm, wet, and heavy, obscuring the windows of the dormitory like plaster glued on the glass. Visibility was zero. That meant 60 wild teenagers would be locked inside all day — which definitely made me want to get outside.

Each summer, the girls dedicated one day of their week to hiking to a tiny hut high on the tundra, manned by a Swiss alpine guide. People overnighted there, using the shelter as a base camp for guided climbs. A stormy day would be perfect for a visit to the guide's cabin. We weren't certain that he would be there because of the bad weather, but we hoped a cup of hot chocolate awaited us. The door would, in any case, be open, providing us shelter and a space to dry out before our return to the barracks.

On the drive up, I'd seen glaciers above me, like fingers combing through the hair of the peaks. They were everywhere — wild, icy, treacherous.

"Will we have to cross any ice?" I asked.

I hadn't brought an ice axe and had no intention of getting near a snow slope or glacier without proper gear.

"Oh, no." Heidi assured me. "We've done this hike for years. Piles of large rocks stacked high in a pyramid shape mark the trail well; the route doesn't come close to the glaciers. "

After a breakfast of muesli and croissants smeared thick with butter and Hero black cherry jam, Appenzeller cheese, and dark coffee, we escaped the raucous teens. The air temperature was warm; it was, after all, the end of July. We wound our way steeply uphill, sweating intensely. The wet snow soaked our anoraks and corduroy knickers. Hiking blind in a world of white, offset only occasionally by the structure of rock markers poking out of the rapidly accumulating snow, was unnerving. Yet I couldn't deny my exhilaration at being out in such calamitous weather. The wind whipped down from the mountains, howling and groaning. The rawness of nature reddened my cheeks.

Bring it on, I silently said to the storm.

We trudged ever upward. The snow filled in our footprints almost as soon as we made them. But it was true, the cairns were massive, perhaps three or four feet high, designed for just such poor visibility days. Ursi called for the first rest stop. We each ate a few squares of chocolate and took a swig from our water bottles. Then we took off our jackets and stuffed them into our small rucksacks—it was just too hot to wear two layers of clothing. Within seconds, our blouses were drenched with melting snow. How ironical that it could be snowing, and we could be so hot; but it was high summer, and we'd been working hard to gain elevation. We switched leads.

I stepped to the front.

I struggled to find the trail beneath the snow. The girls bowed their heads to protect their faces from the pummeling of the wind-driven flakes and followed in my footsteps. Everything was white—the trail, the rocks, the air, our hair, our clothes, our eyelashes.

And then it happened: I felt a change beneath my feet and looked down. Instead of solid ground, I saw fractured ice beneath the covering of fresh precipitation. I was no longer on the supposedly "safe" trail. I was standing on the tongue of a glacier, the place where it ended in a waterfall of menacing cracks. Ice-coated cairns stood mockingly behind me and far off ahead, signaling a safety that the storm had stolen away. The trail dipped downhill below the glacier's terminus and climbed steeply back up on the far side. But I had gone straight—straight and halfway across a glacier that was not supposed to be there. Gray crevasses streaked out in all directions, sleekly hidden by the thick layer of fresh snow.

I stood in a death zone.

My heart drummed madly. I was in the lead. I walked onto the glacier in the whiteout as my friends blindly followed. Bone chilling guilt followed shock.

How could I have made such a dreadful, deadly mistake?

The miniscule daisy pattern on Heidi's wet cotton shirt created a momentary diversion for my brain. The world was filled with tiny, pink daisies, and I wanted to escape into that field of flowers. A gust of humid wind slapped me back to reality, to palpable fear. I did not want to budge, not even expand my lungs to take a breath for fear that the shift in weight would suck me into a crevasse. Our flimsy rucksacks held no life-saving devices—no ropes, no ice axes, no radios, no clothing but for our drenched jackets.

A far-off, haunted look filled Ursi's eyes; she seemed like a deer that had been startled and was about to dart away. The previous summer she had watched her two best friends, roped together, slide from near the summit of a mountain over a cliff to their deaths. She was still suffering from PTSD. Her silence signaled a terrible warning.

Heidi and I debated about the safer escape.

"Heidi, I was in the lead, I should be the one to go first. I could crawl on all fours to spread out my weight and use one arm like an ice axe to probe for crevasses."

"Barbi, this is all my fault," she said in her sing-song, Swiss accent. "I told you there was no glacier. I thought the glacier was far above us. No, I must go first." She started crying.

"Absolutely not! You have two babies, Heidi," I countered.

We considered our options. We knew that the snow held us coming across, but we also knew our combined weight in each footstep could have weakened it; we might break through on the way back. If we went forward, probing as best we could with each step, we might reach the moraine on the far side more quickly. It appeared to be slightly closer.

No words from Ursi. Our battle to make the right choice eluded her in her trauma state. She gazed into the blank, wet haze. The snow fog lifted momentarily, giving us a view of the terrain. The space between us and the higher cairn was riddled with cracks. Now it appeared the only way out was back the way we came, over our trail, which was filling in rapidly with fresh snow.

Heidi moved. She leaned on her right leg—a slight shift, as subtle as a butterfly flapping its wings just once. She didn't even take a step, yet she vanished into the glacier. A black hole no bigger than a dinner plate inhaled her through the ice. There was no sign of the woman who stood before me a split second earlier.

Silence. Ursi remained wordless. Even the storm quieted.

Heidi's disappearance was inconceivable. The glacier swallowed her whole. I held my breath and wished it weren't so, wished I could wake from this nightmare and see her lovely smile.

Then anger welled—anger at myself, anger at the universe.

How could I have let this happen? My god, what have I done?

The storm snarled and snapped me back to my senses. Adrenaline filled my body. Was I standing on a snow bridge that would give way just as it had with Heidi? The thought of movement horrified me, setting off tremors in my legs. It seemed a lifetime of fear passed before I was able to speak and call down:

"Heidi, can you hear me? Heidi!"

Silence.

"Heidi, are you there?"

Did I hear a faint sound, deep in the gut of the glacier—a little, sparrow chirp? I looked to Ursi. She was still staring across the glacier at the cairn on the other side, deaf and mute.

"Barbi. I'm here," came Heidi's voice from her frozen tomb. "My upper body is wedged between the two walls of the crevasse, but my legs are dangling in space; there is nothing but black emptiness beneath my legs. I am going to melt through the ice and die."

I was wildly relieved to hear her voice, but realized that although the narrowing, v-shaped walls of the crevasse had caught her upper body, she could lose her tenuous hold on life at any second. I dropped to my hands and knees, planting my face at the black hole already growing smaller as the snow filled it.

Maybe I can reach in and grasp her hand in mine and hold her safe. Maybe Ursi and I can pull her out.

"How far down do you think you are?"

Maybe we could attach our rucksacks and lower them for her to grab onto, or maybe we could tie our two jackets together and lower them to her.

My desperation conceived desperate plans.

"I think maybe seven or eight meters."

Oh my god. 20 or 30 feet down, totally beyond reach.

I wanted to keep her talking, to keep her hoping. I wanted our voices to be a rope of sound binding us together.

Taking stock of the situation from the information that wept up to the surface, it seemed it could barely be worse: She was wedged deep in a crevasse held only by the tension of the ice on her upper body. The fall ripped the buttons from her blouse leaving her bare skin exposed to the cold. I recently read that a person could not survive more than 45 minutes under those conditions. I checked my watch. 45 minutes would be just about noon. She had knocked out her front teeth. She thought she might have broken an arm and a leg. She was bleeding profusely.

She doesn't have 45 minutes.

And then Ursi bolted.

It wasn't so much that I experienced Ursi leaving as that I experienced her absence. The sense of her disappearance tapped me on the back and distracted me from my agonizing communication with Heidi. Still on my knees, I looked over my left shoulder. In the place where Ursi had stood I saw nothing but snow. I looked over my right shoulder.

Halfway between me and the distant cairn ran a tiny, ghostly figure, translucent in the mist. She ran straight toward the cairn, taking no heed of what was underfoot, making no effort to dodge crevasses.

Time slowed; I stopped breathing. Although she weighed only 100 pounds, there would be snow bridges that could not hold her weight. "Ursi" I screamed into the whiteness. My voice evaporated in the wind. Tiny black footsteps marked her trail as she sprinted furiously for solid ground. I expected at any instant to watch her vanish just as Heidi had done. I fully believed I would never see her again. I saw myself alone out on the ice, trapped in the middle of the glacier as both of them died. The emptiness of being alone on that glacier seemed worse than death itself.

And then she was gone — but not into a crevasse. She made it to the rocks of the lateral moraine and vanished up the trail. That she survived stunned me; that she disappeared in such a state of mental instability terrified me.

Clearly Ursi was headed for the guide's hut, but would she ever find it in the blizzard? How long would it take her to get there? Most critically, would the guide be there? Did he have some kind of radio that could transmit through the storm?

What will I do when Heidi dies?

"Heidi, Ursula has crossed the ice safely and has gone for help to the hut. They'll be back soon, and you *are* going to make it." I lied as much for my own sanity as for Heidi's need for hope.

"Barbi, I'm going to melt the ice and slide through. I'm bleeding so much. I'm going to die. What will happen to my babies? Promise me you will take care of my babies."

Take care of her babies?

I promised, trying to imagine how I could possibly raise two children. But I promised anyway.

"Heidi, you *will* live to watch your daughters grow into beautiful women."

Lying on my stomach, I talked nonstop into that damned hole. I believed that if I could make her continue to talk, I could keep her conscious. I said anything I could think of that was positive and hopeful although I believed none of it. I melded with the whiteness as the fresh snow covered my body. I caught a glimpse of my fancy Swiss watch, snow piling up on the face in a little pyramid, ticking away the minutes of Heidi's life.

50 minutes had passed. My eyes ached wickedly, straining to see through the storm, to see help arriving. Miraculously Heidi was still responding. I felt no cold. Numbness had taken over Heidi's body as well; surely she was in shock. What forces had her body marshaled to keep her alive and conscious so long?

And then, in the distance, I thought I saw movement. At first it seemed a hallucination. Time and place had long since become surreal. But, yes, two snow-caked shadows — a large figure with a big pack and a tiny woman — were moving downhill. The bearded man looked powerful; his strength assuaged my sense of helplessness.

"Heidi. They're coming. The guide is tying a rope around Ursi's waist to belay her across. Heidi, keep talking to me. We're going to get you out, *schatz*."

Weakness made her response almost inaudible, but I could tell she was crying. So was I.

Ursula probed her way toward me with an ice axe the guide brought for her, using the exact route she took when she ran for help. Several minutes passed before she finally reached me because she kept encountering crevasses, crevasses she had previously dashed over in her escape that she now needed to maneuver around.

Ursi then belayed the guide across. As he neared, I took a good look at the man I prayed would be able to help save her life. He had a thick, ice-coated beard. Icicles formed on his mustache and eyebrows. His red mountaineering jacket had the name Hans Ruh engraved on the pocket above a white Swiss cross with a red background. He set down his huge, red pack and immediately started opening the hole with the blunt end of his ice axe. He said nothing to me.

Heidi panicked as heavy snow fell on her head. She started screaming.

"Heidi, it's okay. We have to open the hole to get you out."

But it wasn't okay. The crevasse was too narrow to allow Hans to descend and tie Heidi into the rope. Even little Ursi would be unable to fit between those narrow ice walls that were holding Heidi ever so tenuously.

"Heidi, can you move your arms?" I yelled.

"Yes, I can."

"OK, listen. We're going to lower the rope. You need to wrap it around your back and under your armpits. Knot it with the best knot you ever tied in your life!"

Impossible. Her hands are frozen solid. Blood loss and shock have drained her ability to think. Even if she ties a good knot, how can she manage to avoid slipping through the rope as we pull her up?

I shouted encouragement and prayed to a god I didn't believe in. On the surface the three of us waited with dread, eyes downcast, lost in our private doubts. Tying that knot took what seemed hours.

"It's done; I'm ready," she whispered, sapped of strength.

Hans set up the ice axes as an anchor, winding the rope around them. We pulled with all our strength. As we inched her upward, Heidi cried out in pain with each tug. She was so heavy, a deadweight. With each yank of the rope, the question — *Will the knot hold?* — plagued us.

Hans told us to hold the rope tightly and moved cautiously to the crack as Heidi's devastated body reached the lip. Her broken femur protruded from her right thigh. Her front teeth were either cracked or missing; shattered glasses sat crumpled on her face. She was covered in blood. The big silent man placed her gently on the blanket and sleeping bag he had pulled from his pack. She sobbed weakly as snow started to cover her pale, frigid skin.

I took her hand. It was limp, blue, and so very cold. Now that she was on the surface, I didn't want hypothermia to kill her. My mind struggled to think of a way to bring her more warmth as we waited for help.

"Heidi, sweetheart. You're safe now. I'm going to lie on top of you to keep you warm until the helicopter comes for you."

I stripped down to my underwear and put every article of clothing I had over her. Almost naked amidst those big snowflakes, I carefully placed my body on top of hers. I willed my body heat to warm her. Hans covered us both with the remainder of the blanket and sleeping bag. The snow melted quickly on my bare head and neck; droplets of water, like the tears I was silently shedding, saturated my hair.

I whispered in her ear:

"I love you, Heidi. Stay awake. The guide called the helicopter. It *is* coming soon. The guide called your husband; he is hiking up now. I love you. Stay with me."

Hans radioed the emergency helicopter the instant Ursi got to the hut. But now we waited on the whims of the storm. Would it steal Heidi's life by preventing the helicopter from reaching us and leave her to die after she had been rescued from the deep ice? The storm had to relent, had to give Heidi the break of a lifetime. I pleaded with the storm to let the helicopter in through the pass to the East.

With my love, I infused my warmth into Heidi as time toyed with her survival. Her breath was shallow. Hans did what he could to stench her bleeding. All color had drained from her skin. She wound in and out of consciousness. We'd been waiting for 40 minutes for the helicopter; two hours had passed since she dropped through the ice. I kept talking.

The storm made a muffled moan. I looked into the snow cloud, toward the sound. Where there had been only undistinguishable whiteness, a helicopter now sat. It had slipped through a hole in the gale, flown blind, and landed on the moraine at the far edge of the glacier. Dark figures rushed out and went to work to reach us. The helicopter was equipped not only with medical emergency equipment, but also with mountain rescue gear. The crew threw boards across the crevasses slowly wending their way to us.

I was still exuding heat when they lifted me from Heidi's body to carry her to the chopper.

And she was still alive.

Heidi was quickly hooked up to an IV and given blood and fluids in the mini-ER sanctuary of the chopper. The hospital communicated with her husband at the barracks to identify her blood type before the rescue bird lifted off. Leave it to the Swiss. Heidi was determined to hang on, but now the problem was the worsening weather. The helicopter could not get out.

It was then I noticed the entire camp of kids — silent, still, and somber. They huddled safely on the trail and watched. Heidi and Ursi's husbands had mounted a rescue expedition in case the chopper couldn't get in and arrived from the barracks with the kids about the same time as the helicopter. They tentatively made their way across the ice toward us, roped, probing with axes.

"Barbi, you should go back now. Heidi is in good hands. There is no more you can do here," said Toni, Heidi's husband.

Ursi and I were guided back across the glacier. Then with students in front of and behind us, we were ushered down to the barracks. I looked back until I could no longer see the helicopter, the glacier, Heidi.

The storm continued to worsen, leaving Heidi trapped. At 10 p.m. she was still stranded and in critical need of expert hospital care. The decision was made to carry her out strapped onto a stretcher to an ambulance waiting on the pass road 2,000 feet below. A dangerous descent was deemed the fastest way down. It took six men — the two husbands, Hans, and three climbing instructors from the camp — three hours in brutal conditions.

Later she told me the whistling of the wind was the only sound she heard in the black night. The trail was blown in with snow. The slope was almost vertical, making the avalanche danger extreme. Cold and hungry, the men moved cautiously in the darkness, bearing Heidi's weight and the burden of her heavy stretcher. They sank up to their hips in the snow, struggling and sweating with effort, blindly feeling for the track underfoot.

Those six experienced mountaineers preparing for the heavy carry pared down their packs, leaving their ropes at the accident site. They departed without a means to safely secure the stretcher on that desperate descent. They tried hard to focus and not stumble. But stumble they did. The group slid and fell three times, dropping Heidi each time and almost losing her to the void. She remained conscious and later talked to me in detail of the horror of sliding unrestrained over the snow in the stormy night.

Heidi lived to see her daughters grow into beautiful women. Her will to survive remains for me the strongest reminder I have of the indomitable nature of the human spirit. Metal screws and plates have held her broken body together all these years. Although she still smiles that lovely smile, she suffers to this day with chronic pain and debilitating arthritis. The events of that experience live in her mind unrelentingly, stealing her sleep and violating her peace. From this she will never be free.

Chapter 10

GRIZZLY

The Snake River, 1986

"Adventures are something you have when you screw up."
~ John Sanford

**My selection of men had always been atrocious.
Whether I was falling in love for the hundredth time or
simply choosing a partner to climb, boat or ski with, I
managed to pick the most undependable, unreliable or
unfaithful guy within reach. On this adventure trip in
Wyoming, my life as a loose cannon led me to
unimaginable consequences.**

I had joined the Rockies Sea Kayak Club a year back. The
closest sea was a thousand miles away; I liked the oxymoron.
Massive reservoirs and a few long rivers in the West made for
great play and travel on water. I enjoyed day trips and week-long
excursions with the group, a fun-loving assortment of scientists,
teachers, lawyers, and such, all with two things in common—a
passion for paddling and a love of wilderness camping.

Our sea kayaks ranged in length from 14 to 21 feet. Most had
rudders for steering with compartments fore and aft for storage of
camping gear, food, clothing, and the requisite portable latrine,

the "boomer." The day trips made for competitive, high-speed sprints around a lake or down a flat river. Yet the camping trips were my favorite.

One summer I paddled to the most distant arm of Yellowstone Lake, one of the most remote places in the continental US. There were no roads, not even dirt roads, in any direction, making the region a true wilderness where wolves and grizzlies thrived. I awoke at night to the howling of a wolf pack and found their prints around my tent in the morning. Another year, also on Yellowstone Lake, I sat mesmerized for hours, watching white pelicans take off from an island sanctuary where they bred and raised their young. They soared into the cobalt heavens, round and round, higher and higher, until they became invisible in the Wyoming sky.

I yearned to be away from civilization and experience one adventure trip after another. That longing seemed the very cloth out of which my being was fashioned. I was in graduate school getting a degree in counseling psychology in 1989 and had the entire summer free. Unfortunately, most of my sports compatriots worked. I put up my antennae for a partner with an equal urge for adventure and the freedom to escape into the wilderness with me. I felt like a shark cruising for prey as I circulated during the club's annual boat fair. My attention vacillated between the cool, new demo kayaks and the cute, single men who might be available.

I guess I could have gone alone, but by then I had spent so much time on my own in the wilderness that the isolation no longer held its original draw: I no longer identified myself as "the lonely one." Over the years, I had also shattered the myth of my childhood that I was weak, helpless, and abandoned. I had proven that I was both strong and independent.

———————

"Wanna look at my new sea kayak, sweetheart? Wanna beer? Got a cooler full right under that tree."

Downriver Dick found me and promptly proceeded to try and pick me up. He might as well have been asking me to come see his etchings. His appearance was acceptable: 5'9", a totally unremarkable but not ugly face, good build and no excess body fat. His brown eyes flashed flirtation. True to form, the invitation immediately sucked me in and led me to spending the day with him, drinking beer, telling paddling tales and taking a spin on the lake, chasing his "fucking awesome" English sea kayak.

Dick was a radiologist, had practiced at the local community hospital, but left that position recently. Did I ever wonder or ask why? Of course not. Instead I thought:

Ah ha, he's unemployed; he's free to play.

He seemed to know how to have a good time and a good laugh. In fact, wasn't it serendipity? He was looking for an adventure partner too.

And so, without knowing anything further about the man, not even why people called him Downriver Dick, I proceeded to lay out my plans for a trip to the Snake River and Jackson Lake in the Tetons. I suggested we paddle a flatwater stretch of the Snake that flowed into the lake, then slowly make our way down the lake's western shoreline, wilderness camping at the foot of those famous mountains. I thought I had baited an enticing hook. He snapped it up all too eagerly as he finished his sixth beer.

I figured we would have a great road trip and kayak adventure and, who knew, maybe a new romance would blossom. I never thought to ask around about his reputation as a boater, no less as a person, yet surmised that a man willing to run off with me on a daring adventure might be a good candidate for a love affair.

One week later he pulled up to my condo in a beat up, old Volvo. He'd insisted on taking his car. Why not? He also insisted on doing all the driving. Fine, I could take in the sights, relax, and read while he drove. I looked into the car. It was messy. Camping paraphernalia, crumpled clothes, cooking gear, garbage—all thrown together in a heap.

I'd neatly piled my gear on the lawn. My lime green sea kayak sat patiently in the grass waiting to get wet. We managed to stuff my belongings into the Volvo. While loading the vehicle I noticed quite a few empty beer cans on the floor. A stale alcoholic scent hung in the car like a damp rain cloud. There were a few bottles of Scotch—full. I spotted several bottles of wine, white and red, amongst his belongings. He noticed me noticing.

"Oh, I see you've discovered that I have the beverages covered. Can't go on a great adventure without great beverages."

We'd agreed to overnight near the Wyoming border in Craig, visiting with Dick's friends. By the time we arrived, a queasy stomach, derived from our interactions, was my other constant companion. No matter what the topic of conversation, he had to disagree with what I said—and he had to be right. Why hadn't he behaved like this the day I met him? I clearly remembered his eagerness to please, his willingness to listen and defer. What happened? The beast had awoken, and the beast definitely had control issues.

By the time we retired to our sleeping bags in the backyard that evening, he had drunk a massive quantity of alcohol. He didn't seem inebriated; I guess that's because his tolerance was so high. He passed out and snored loudly enough to keep me awake most of the night.

I lay under the stunning Colorado stars and fretted. I just didn't get it, this guy thing. Didn't your relationship with your father have something to do with the men you chose? My father wasn't an alcoholic; he barely drank. However, he did have rage and control issues. I spent my childhood trying to please him, always failing. But how did that get me enmeshed with people like Downriver Dick?

The following day, quiet pervaded the drive north. I found the way to avoid his power ploys was to avert conversation. And Dick? Dick was hung over big time. That kept him still.

As the hours flew by, the warm Rocky Mountain sun heated up the cool environment inside the vehicle. We left the ranch lands of northwest Colorado behind for the dull, monochromatic landscape of southern Wyoming. The barren, arid terrain hid vast riches of gas and oil beneath its surface. Small herds of well-camouflaged antelope scoured the high desert for bits of sustenance as tumble weed drifted across the highway in the ubiquitous wind.

Finally, I spotted the Wind River Range peeking up from the high plains to the northeast, a sure sign that we were approaching the exquisite North Country. As we left the desert, massive green cottonwoods appeared. A river sparkled, reminding me that we were going paddling and just how much I cherished being on the water. A pair of golden eagles soared overhead as a prairie dog played chicken in the road. Dick held the steering wheel in one hand and a can of beer in the other. At least he was a good driver, even half looped.

On our way through the Park, I insisted that we check out the conditions with the River Ranger at the Teton National Park Visitors' Center. Downriver Dick strolled in behind me. He couldn't allow me to gather vital information and then have me relay it to him; he had to hear it with his own ears. This time I didn't blame him for wanting control. This was critical information.

"Oh, that's a beautiful stretch of wilderness. You'll love it," the female ranger said. "There are two pretty serious things to be aware of though. First, you'll be in prime grizzly habitat, so you'll want to be watching for bears along the river's edge. When you stop, be sure to use strict bear etiquette. You know the rules?"

"Yup," we chimed in simultaneously.

"OK. Then the other thing. Listen closely, guys. This is *really* important. Heavy snows blanketed the region last winter. The spring flooding was extensive. The Snake overflowed its banks, took out some big trees, created new channels. A vicious strainer now sits across a minor fork of the river. You get caught in that strainer, you die. In fact, we lost a young woman there five days ago."

A strainer is an object, frequently a tree, which has fallen over a river, blocking the passage of solid things while allowing the river to crash through. If a kayak hits a strainer, the hydraulics pin the boat against the tree. The boater drowns because the force of the current prevents escape.

"So here's the deal. You will reach a point on river right where you see a cliff band running north/south. You can't miss those cliffs. They are the first and only cliffs you will encounter. You will then come to a confusing junction. It looks like the main river goes straight and the fork to the left peters out. But you *must* take the left fork. You may even have to walk your boats down the left fork because it widens and gets shallow and rocky. The branch that goes straight turns a bend and narrows radically. The current picks up, you go around several curves, and you end up in the strainer. Any questions?"

Sounds pretty damn clear to me.

"Ok. Have a great paddle. Be safe. Remember, take the left fork."

At the end of the day, we pulled into the most northerly campsite on Jackson Lake in Teton National Park. The dampness of the early evening roused me from my dreamy, on-the-road reverie. We were back where I had survived my first mountaineering adventures. A dusty mauve haze hung over the water. Etheric columns of pale smoke rose from campfires being set for the evening. The air was still, the alpenglow an apricot haze over the dusty purple peaks. We lucked out, finding a campsite away from the others with a view of the placid water.

It had been a long day. I had the wisdom to bring my own tent on that trip. I crawled in as a coyote howled a greeting to the oncoming night. Downriver Dick sat fondling a bottle of Jack Daniels in front of his tent as I fell asleep to a cricket lullaby.

———————

The alarm startled me awake before sunrise. The night had been frosty cold. I threw on hat, gloves, and all the clothes I could find, preparing for our departure. I was more than ready to get onto the water and into the wilderness.

Everything will be fine once I dip my paddle in the Snake.

We drove north toward Yellowstone National Park. Finally we crossed a bridge over the icy, silent river. The parking lot, where rafters took out from the whitewater rapids upriver and boaters put in for our flatwater paddle, sat just off the highway bordered by tall, dark pines. The Snake, draining the Yellowstone wilderness, was running cold and swift, but the surface was still, a moving mirror. The water was so clear that every detail on the river's pebbly bottom could be seen. A white cloud of ice fog hung above it. We were alone.

We unloaded the boats, both 17 feet long, sleek, tippy, and fast. We loaded them with water, food, and camping gear, donning our life vests. The weather report promised a gorgeous day. I knew that once the sun rose above the surrounding peaks, the world would warm, the birds would sing.

The water was moving swiftly, so I floated downriver not paddling, using my rudder pedals to steer. The forest was so still, the morning so pristine, that I wished I could slow my boat down; I wanted to draw the day out. A bald eagle flew low over our kayaks, headed downriver.

Take the left fork, I whispered to it.

DD was ahead of me; of course he insisted on being first. Every minute took us deeper into the wild and deeper into grizzly country. I kept my eyes peeled. I had no idea of how a grizzly would react to a boater or to churning paddles. The river was not so deep or wide that a grizzly couldn't jump in and pounce on the boat. I could not remember ever reading of an encounter between a grizzly and a kayak. Yet I was nervous and justifiably so.

The sun broke over the mountains to the east, bringing with it a pure, pale light. The forest shifted to a warmer hue, the shadows went from black to blue. Rays of sun breaking through the trees slowly tempered the frigid cold emanating from the river. I heard a birdsong I could not identify, but I imagined it was singing good morning to me. I was honored to be moving through this wilderness sanctuary, happy to be alive, one with nature. I drifted along that morning, juggling joy with my concern of bears, keeping a sharp lookout for those critical cliffs.

I saw the cliffs.

Surely these are the cliffs.

They weren't up against the river's bank, but perhaps a quarter mile away, yet exactly as the ranger described them. I felt instant panic: Dick had gotten way ahead of me. He seemed oblivious, slouching down in his seat, watching the world go by. His paddle lay across his lap, perpendicular to his boat, indicating that he wasn't about to pull over to the water's edge or make a quick turn to the left, to safety, when the river branched. I wondered how long we had before that fork appeared.

"Dick," I yelled, breaking the perfect silence in what had been a perfect morning. "Dick, pull out. I see the cliffs."

No response. Downriver Prick was playing stubborn. Again, I yelled. He didn't change posture. I sprinted hard and caught up with him.

Pulling alongside his boat, I was about to start raving when he said authoritatively: "Those are *not* the cliffs. They're too far away."

An icy chill swept through me. We were embarking on another power struggle, one that could kill us both. He was so damn determined to be the expert and make the decisions.

I considered what to do if the fork were around the next bend. If I stayed behind him going down the wrong fork, perhaps I could somehow jump onto shore soon enough to avoid the strainer and reach out with a paddle from the bank to try to save him. Unlikely. But if I forked left, I would be leaving him to die.

And then the fork was visible ahead of us.

Please, no, not so soon.

On the left a shallow channel disappeared into the brush. Rivulets of water trickled around bleached stones that filled a gap between stands of tall willows guarding the passage. We'd have to carry our boats, walking down the rocks, to go that way. The deep, powerful current ran straight ahead, looking very much like the only real option.

But that's exactly the way the river ranger described it. We're here; we must veer left.

"Oh, God, Dick, please. This is exactly the way she described it. Please go left."

"You're wrong. That couldn't possibly be the way; it's a dead end. It must be farther down. Relax, woman."

In the next heartbeat *we* were past the escape route. I had made my choice: I simply couldn't leave him to drown.

The river narrowed, turning an ominous, black onyx. Suddenly the current picked up perceptibly. Back paddling did nothing to slow me down. The channel began snaking, making it impossible to see what was around each curve. With every bend I feared we would plow right into the strainer. I kept my distance from Dick's boat as best I could. Dense willows and alders overhung the bank on river left, creating an impassable wall. Suddenly the right bank rose up turning into a 20-foot high cliff, making that side of the river inescapable. With the acceleration of the current, we were covering distance rapidly.

"Do you hear that?" shouted Dick.

I did hear something crashing, like violent surf pounding on cliffs.

"It's the strainer," I shouted back. "It must be huge to be making that much noise."

Dick spied a tiny eddy, an area of calm water where the left bank jutted out slightly. The water doubled back on itself in a circular motion behind the bank. With a deft maneuver of his paddle, he twirled his kayak around and drove his boat into the eddy, facing upstream. An eddy is the only way to exit a fast river; it's the kayaker's safe haven.

The eddy wasn't big enough to fit two sea kayaks. My heart pounded riotously. I didn't know if the roaring I heard was inside or outside my head. Dick was safe, but where could I go? In a few seconds I would be flying by him. The strainer was around the next bend.

I watched Dick slide up to the bank, jump out of his boat, and lift it onto shore. He did this in a heartbeat, then ran a few yards down the shoreline. As I passed his boat, I planted my paddle, spun my boat around, and maneuvered toward the bank where he stood, ready to grab my boat. Dick had just saved my life.

I extricated myself from the cockpit and slithered onto the bank. We pulled my boat onto the shore. We stared into each other's terrified eyes, two adrenaline junkies close to overdosing. The noise of the strainer sounded like the roar of a small Niagara Falls.

"Look," he pointed to the ground between the river and the tall willow wall, "There's a trail here. Let's walk downriver and have a look at the strainer." The trail was muddy and full of grizzly prints. Huge claw marks punctuated the dirt.

We walked single file down this bear route, over a hump, and around a corner. The strainer appeared before us — deafening, defying any chance of passage or escape. The river was being sucked under the tree, agitating like a giant washing machine. The force was palpable. The strainer was a monstrous nest of wood and debris. We stood, hypnotized. I had to give Dick credit for his lightening-quick reaction, for being there when I really needed him most.

As we started the walk back, I contemplated the situation we now found ourselves in — alive and stuck in the wilderness in bear country. I was looking down at my feet as I crested the hump in the trail. Suddenly things were happening fast again. Dick, 10 feet ahead of me, yelled "GRIZZLY!", sprinted for his boat, pushed it into the water, and pulled away from the shoreline. Still facing upstream, he was protected by the hydraulics of the eddy. It allowed him to sit near the eddy line where the downriver water and the circulating eddy met. He sat very still, eyes darting between the approaching bear and me.

A grizzly boar thrashed through the willows, headed for the trail I stood on. He hadn't heard us yet because of the strainer noise. The wind blew downstream, so he hadn't smelled us either. But he was coming. His head was massive, his fur rich and silver-tipped. The boar's paws were the size of frying pans, the claws as long as my fingers.

I was trapped between the grizzly and the strainer.

In those split seconds of primal decision-making, I knew one thing. I knew I would not lie down on the trail, curl into a ball, and play dead, the recommended behavior if you couldn't back away safely. I knew I would not have that monster scalp me with his claws and maul me to death; I would not die that way.

I snapped into action, exploding toward my kayak like a greyhound out of the gate. There was a slim chance that I might save myself on the water if I could pull off a tricky whitewater maneuver under near impossible circumstances.

Damn, I'm going to try.

Two weeks earlier, on a club paddle, one of the guys asked me if I knew how to ferry. No, I had never heard of it. He then gave me the lesson that could save my life. I learned to face my ultra-long kayak upriver into the current and place it exactly at the right angle, then paddle like hell. A perfect angle caused the boat to move *across* the river, preventing the kayak from being swept downriver by the flow. Practicing the technique on a big, slow-moving river was easy, fun. The ferry I now needed to pull off was a life/death maneuver: If I got it wrong, I died.

The grizzly stepped out of the willows and stopped as I pushed off from the shore and started paddling with fury. I stroked hysterically, my paddle like a windmill blade in a thunderous current of air. I knew the motion would attract the bear, but I wasn't going to let the black water claim me either. The grizzly rose on its hind legs, trying with its poor vision to make out what the commotion was on the river. God, he was huge.

My ferry was working. But within seconds I was on the opposite side of the narrow channel, the side with the 20-foot high, undercut wall. Roots from the trees that stood on top of the cliff stuck out of the yellow mud of the wall, taunting me:

"Look, we're right here, and you can't grab us to save yourself."

I realized I would have to reverse the ferry and head back toward the bear that was now walking down the trail, beady eyes looking pointedly in my direction as his wet, black nose twitched incessantly.

At the rate I was moving, the bear and I were going to arrive at the same spot on the shoreline simultaneously.

Focus on your ferry. Your ferry is the key to your survival.

As I neared the bear, I made a decision. I would not look to my right at him. If he was going to lunge, I would know it soon enough. Instead I watched the angle of my boat, then Dick's face, then the angle of my boat. I knew Dick's expression would switch from dread to horror if the bear made a move.

I could feel the beast's bulk looming as I neared the bank; I could smell his strong, musky spoor. Surely, now, he could also smell me, my panic, my terror.

Don't look; don't look!

I pointed the nose of the kayak left again and started to ferry away, desperate yet prepared for the worst. It was then that I saw a change in Dick's expression. His face turned from frozen to animated, filled with relief. I couldn't look over my shoulder to confirm that the beast was continuing down the trail. If I let the boat's nose drift a degree too far, the river would have swept the boat around, driving me down toward both the strainer *and* the bear.

I finished the left ferry and aggressively ferried right. This time instead of a bear at the shoreline, Dick was there to grab the boat. The bear was gone, or so we dearly hoped. I could barely draw myself out of the kayak. I collapsed on the ground, face in the dirt, spent.

"What are we going to do? That bear could come back. This place is infested with bears. The fork we need to reach is so far away, and there's no way to get there." Rage and hysteria upstaged my brief collapse.

"What the hell are we going to do, Dick, Mr. Smartass, Know It All, Always Right? Huh?" I screamed.

The brush seemed impenetrable. Yet our only answer was to bushwhack back upriver. How would I ever find the energy to haul myself and my heavy, loaded boat through thickets, over hummocks, and around blockades of vegetation?

Whenever I could, I dragged or pushed the boat, but mostly I needed to lift it over my head to propel it forward. The willows were five to six feet high; my boat weighed 54 pounds empty. As I ripped and tore through the vegetation, it ripped and tore back. Before long I was dripping blood from cuts and scratches. I stumbled and fell repeatedly, sustaining dozens of bruises. It seemed that the brush was alive, pulling me down, bashing me, brutalizing me. I kept looking over my shoulder, praying that the bear hadn't backtracked, hoping it wasn't stalking us.

Time wore on. Enveloped in fury, I was suffering from the crazy-making buzz of mosquitoes.

Why wouldn't he listen to me? Almost got me killed. Twice. Bear and strainer. And now we are thrashing through the wilderness making a racket. Every bear between Yellowstone and the Tetons will hear us.

Some hours later we arrived at the place where we should have veered left. I stumbled down the wet rocks to a muddy, level patch that wasn't overrun with willows. The muck was full of grizzly tracks. I collapsed onto some clods of grass, sweating, bloody, filthy. All I could think of was getting my kayak on the river, effortlessly floating out to Jackson Lake, and paddling back to our campsite. A multi-day trip with Downriver Dick was definitely out.

Getting down the slow-moving branch of the Snake and paddling the lake, whipped wild with a harsh, afternoon headwind, took several more hours. The day seemed so unfair, one immense challenge after another. To get back to that campground demanded a determination and a toughness very few people would ever muster. The bow of my boat rose up on the waves, then crashed hard into the troughs, jarring my bones, saturating my body with cold water. I put my head down and dug deep, deep enough to make it back… again.

The paddle trip I took was generally a very easy and lovely wilderness excursion. The conditions that particular year coupled with interpersonal dynamics led to near disaster. I just never knew what life had in store when I took off on those escapades — or how lucky I could be.

This story is really about personal forgiveness and love, about arriving at a point in my life when I could look at the poor choices I made and forgive myself for them, understanding with compassion just how human I am.

While the men I picked to be partners in my adventures and my life turned out decade after decade to be big mistakes, there were so many others who supported me, befriended me and mentored me. Those are the men I will love forever. Some have died, some have vanished, some still call me every week, and one married me in 2004. I am a very fortunate woman.

Chapter 11

SEEKING
THE SACRED JAGUAR

Belize, 1996

"I am open to the guidance of synchronicity and do not let expectations hinder my path."
~ Dali Lama

The jungle night tossed restlessly against the heavens. Huge, black, moisture-laden clouds tumbled down the Maya Mountains and crossed the tropical wilderness as they headed toward the sea. The breeze stirred the high canopy; it whispered of all that is dangerous and deadly in the dark.

It was midnight. I shouldered my backpack, slipped out of the safety of the compound, lit my pencil-thin flashlight and silently walked to the rutted double-track I would take eastward. The time had come to seek the jaguar.

Life was grand. I had succeeded in creating just about the best of all possible worlds: I had an advanced degree in counseling psychology; a meaningful professional life geared toward the helping of women in need of psychological support; a stage presence as both a facilitator of divorce-recovery classes and a presenter of self-designed, personal-growth seminars entitled "In Search of Self"; an active, competitive sports life; built-in time for travel adventures. I even found my soul mate and lived for a few years with the man of my dreams before he found the woman of *his* dreams, leaving me to strike out as a single female once again. Nothing new about that…

In the beginning the symptoms snuck up on me—periods of GI tract problems, a bladder inflammation, dropping my pen repeatedly as I sat in session with a patient, frequent bouts of fatigue attributed to my non-stop lifestyle and aggressive sports-training regimen.

But then, one night in early autumn, I awoke in a bath of sweat. My long hair was drenched in perspiration as were the pillows and the sheets. A terrible headache clamped my brain in its vice. The arteries on the sides of my head throbbed with pain; my vision blurred. Waves of nausea washed over me; vomiting and diarrhea followed. Too ill to clean up the bathroom, I barely made it back to bed before I passed out.

Light gently penetrated white gauze curtains, but it felt too intense to tolerate; the smallest sounds seemed like wildly loud intrusions into my nervous system. Weakness held me down as I tried to rise from the bed; dizziness accompanied me into the bathroom where I found the mess I left the night before. I could not remember what happened.

So tired, so confused. The phone sat in the living room. I crawled out of bed and tried to get there. I walked my hands along the wall, unable to balance without assistance. Halfway through the condo, a tiredness like thick mist descending on a moor enveloped me. I lay down on the carpet in a fetal position, unable to take another step.

What am I doing on the floor? Why can't I think straight?

I slipped into a long sleep on that rug, lost to the world. The mystery disease that tiptoed through my life when my love relationship fell apart now pounded on my brain like a sledgehammer.

After a week of indescribable fatigue and severe mental confusion, getting to a doctor seemed very necessary but barely feasible. I had tremors, an incessant headache with stiff neck, muscle and joint aches, and pains from head to toe. Fevers and chills racked my body. The glands in my neck were so swollen that I looked like I had the mumps. I had never been fragile in such a way. Cognitive impairment and disorientation left me afraid to leave the house. When I did try to go to the doctor, I realized that I didn't know how to find my way. I couldn't even figure out how to get to the Safeway three blocks from my place to replenish food stocks. I knew many people superficially, yet I did not have a true friend to call on.

Eventually I managed medical consultations, but no one could figure out what was wrong with me. I was tested for everything from malaria to AIDS. The head of the MS Center in Denver told me there was a 50% chance that MS was the culprit. As I carefully maneuvered my way out of that waiting room, I looked at the patients, each one sitting in a wheel chair, and decided *my* condition would not be MS. I did not return for the spinal tap the doctor ordered.

I survived the brain inflammation and started to manage my most basic needs. Yet all my systems were faltering and symptoms battered me like a pro boxer pounding on a novice fighter who didn't belong in the ring. The impossibility of returning to my practice added insult to injury. I told my patients I was taking a long-term sabbatical. If I couldn't think, I couldn't work.

Where was there to go when traditional medicine failed? My primary doc was an integrative MD, so alternative medicine was a part of his bag of tricks, but it failed me as well. I tried local healers, essential oils, meditation, sound therapy. I even saw a swami visiting the States from India who had reputedly performed miracles. $500 poorer and with the healer's statement:

"You are a very sick woman; I can do no more."

I walked away from the guru *shtick*.

The longer I was ill, the more intuitive I became. Thoughts began to think me. That was a good thing because my cognition was as badly strained as an Alzheimer patient. I realized that I needed to leave the US and find a healing environment in which to live. It had to be a place where the medicine was actually part of the world — so, a rainforest, the best pharmacy on the planet. It had to be a place with an ocean because my inner voice told me the ocean would take me back to my cellular origins in the sea and heal me. It had to be a place where there was a thriving tradition of *curanderos*, healers, herbalists. I scoured the world map, did extensive research on healing in native cultures and decided it had to be Belize.

A remission/relapse pattern set in. My "remissions" left me plenty tired and sick, but capable of some activity. It was October, and I was on my feet a little each day. I figured I'd better get myself to Belize before I couldn't. Within a week I was flying over the Caribbean to the endless jungles of Central America.

I headed toward a place with ancient roots, a wild and empty world that promised healing from the earth itself. As the jet descended, impenetrable jungles blanketed the mountains, swamps devoid of habitation covered the lowlands, and the waters inside the second longest reef on the planet sparkled an irresistible Caribbean aquamarine.

The taxi driver took me into the center of Belize City, a small, somewhat shabby tropical port that had long since seen its glory days. I spied vestiges of the British colonial period as we neared the waterfront. The country had only gained its independence from the Brits in 1981. Before the day was out I saw most of the peoples who made Belize their home: Creoles, Garifuna, Mestizos, East Indians, Lebanese, Chinese, Mennonites, Guatemalans, and Hondurans. The Maya claimed the honor of being the only indigenous folk; I would not see them until I entered the interior later in my stay.

At the simple pension I had selected from my guidebook, a two-story, lush violet vine charmed me, but the stench of open sewage canals stopped me short. While some water treatment plants existed, many of the citizens still dumped their honey pots into canals that crisscrossed the city.

In the morning I made my way to the wharf and boarded a high-speed water taxi, a large speedboat that serviced the cayes along the barrier reef. I was hungry for the tropical ocean experience and chose Caye Caulker as my home base. It was a 50-minute, 20-mile boat ride and the least expensive location I could find to live.

The boat slammed into four-foot seas with tremendous force, shuddered with the impact, and rattled my brain. Although drenched and a bit nauseous from the fumes of the engine by the time we docked, I was high on the salt water spray, the smell of the ocean, and the maritime breeze. Living surrounded by the sea seemed a very good plan indeed.

Caye Caulker was a limestone coral island once used by pirates. It measured just one mile wide by five miles long, most of it scrub jungle and mangroves. It highest point was eight feet above sea level. As I reached the main "street," stretching along its east side, I exclaimed out loud to no one in particular:

"This is the tropical paradise of my dreams."

Palms filled with coconuts swayed between gaily painted shacks while exotic birds gossiped in the deciduous trees. A small sailboat breezed along on the protected waters inside the reef. The sun flicked diamond light off each wave. Colossal white clouds perched far off on the horizon. With the land and sea at almost the same level, I felt as though I stood in both realms simultaneously.

A sign announced: "Go Slow," the motto of the place. The caye was a tropical botanical garden; profuse, large flowers in every imaginable shade scented the air. Mangy, scrawny dogs called potlickers by the locals roamed the streets looking for handouts and garbage. Reggae music drifted happily from boom boxes. I saw my first, real Rastafarian. The sweet smell of pot mingled with the salt air. Caye Caulker epitomized hippy heaven.

"Café Espresso" read the sign at one of the brightly colored shacks.

"Welcome. Come in. Make yourself at home," said Cindy, a twenty-something woman with hazel, feline eyes.

Cindy was a beautiful, open-hearted girl who would become a wonderful friend and provide deep emotional and spiritual support during my stay. I asked her where I might find my landlords, and she pointed the way.

With key in hand, I climbed the stairs to the second-floor apartment of a dilapidated, board house, my new home. I entered a sparsely furnished living room but was immediately drawn outside by a spacious deck overlooking the town, the celeste bay, the reef, and the deep blue ocean. The view left me breathless! The tops of palm trees brushed at the deck's railings, and giant frigate birds, their iridescent black feathers glimmering in the sunlight, rode updrafts far above my head.

I could live here for the rest of my life.

Back at Cindy's I asked: "Where's the best place to swim?"

She warned me away from the mangrove swamps: "We have a healthy population of saltwater crocodiles." Then she directed me to a lovely white sand beach, the in-town swimming hangout.

As I walked there, I noticed that the ugliest dog I had ever laid eyes on followed me.

I spread my blanket on the sand. With snorkel and goggles in place, I flowed into the shallow, languid water and floated face down, watching little tropical fish dancing in the mild currents. In my mind I repeated my new mantra as I became one with the sea: *Heal, heal.*

The first night held surprises. Several varieties of mosquitoes, including the tiny, dive-bombing ones that carried malaria, arrived on cue as the sun made its glorious end-of-day dip below the horizon. I was prepared with one of the most indispensable products required on the island: mosquito coils. The toxic smell was nearly intolerable, but it did keep those critters away.

Loud noises jarred me awake not long after I passed out from exhaustion. Had I locked the door; was someone breaking in? Yes and no. The noises were around the apartment and inside the walls and cabinets.

Rats don't climb up to second-story apartments, do they?

I lit my flashlight and stepped into the kitchen. Cockroaches the size of mice scurried in all directions, leaving my skin crawling. So much for a good night's sleep.

Welcome to Central America, Barbara.

A day-glow orange sit-on-top kayak carried me toward the reef early the next morning. The rhythm of the paddle strokes hypnotized me as I watched large, brilliantly tinted fish, highlighted by the white sand bottom, swim below. The breeze barely whispered, leaving the protected waters inside the reef dead flat. I saw not a single fishing boat, dive boat, or sailboat; I was alone in a magical water world. I headed for a break in the reef, knowing that a deep channel would provide the most variety for underwater gazing. I also had no doubt that there were plenty of dangerous sharks cruising the trough.

An hour later I reached the reef; tied the long, plastic cord attached to the bow around my waist; connected the paddle and water bottle with a bungee cord to the boat. I donned my hot pink snorkel, mask, and fins (which matched my hot pink bikini) and jumped in. I placed my face in the warm water and looked down at the world I had come to visit. With arms at my sides, I kicked my legs from the hip and began a voyage of exquisite sensory experience.

Awe of the aqueous wonderland replaced my fear of being alone as a show of vibrant colors and shapes made me feel I was on psychedelics. Countless schools of fish swam, floated, and darted about. I read that 500 species of fish lived there and marveled that I could be in the midst of such a vital world, the sea altar of the Belize Barrier Reef. A magnificent Queen Angel Fish peered out from behind an orange-shaded coral fan. Sunlight sketched a striped, glittering pattern in the water as it pierced the surface. A savage-looking Moray eel suddenly snaked its speckled body out of a hidden hole, mouth open, sharp little teeth threatening. Poisonous sea urchins covered the floor like black polka dots. Coral in unimaginable shapes, colors, and sizes moved, breathed, fed.

I snorkeled along blissfully until the reef turned a corner. Suddenly I peered down thirty or forty feet into a trench where the water glowed an exquisite shade of azure to match the color of the coral below. Gazing into the deep cut was like looking into some sort of underwater prism. I saw Elkhorn Coral and, deeper yet, Staghorn Coral and gargantuan Brain Coral. I diligently watched for sharks. If a curious one appeared, I hoped to jump into the kayak before it took a bite out of me to test if I was suitable lunch fare. The underwater visibility was endless; I could see a shark from a long way off.

As the water became rougher, a little voice inside my head warned me not to travel beyond the shelter of the reef. For once, I listened to my own counsel and turned back.

Inside the reef's protection I realized that I had been out for hours and knew I had to return. Low blood sugar, dehydration, sunburn, fatigue, and a steady breeze made the paddle back extremely taxing. Yet I felt as if spending the day at the reef was the very kind of experience that would contribute to my healing.

How could absorbing so much life and so much beauty not make me well?

Another ride on the brain-blender water taxi dropped me back in the city. The stench from the canals accosted me again, but even so the place began to grow on me. I roamed the streets, taken by the amazing cultural diversity.

The tantalizing smell of sawdust filled rows of woodworking stalls. Men hauled hand-pulled carts stacked high with chairs and dressers down the narrow streets. I'd meandered into the Prussian Mennonite quarter. That Anabaptist group migrated, 3,000 strong, from Pennsylvania to Belize in 1959 to escape modern society. Those in Belize City were carpenters who created elegant, sturdy furniture sold throughout the country. The women astounded me. They stood around in the same costume that their forbearers wore four hundred years ago: a long, heavy plaid dress; thick, black stockings; ugly, laced shoes with a fat, lifted heel, and a bonnet tied with a bow. And I was hot in my sleeveless top and shorts!

I sought out the Belize City Market based on Cindy's information that the most renowned herbal healer in the country had a booth there. A cavernous, high-ceilinged wooden structure housed the market. Merchants sold everything: wares, arts and crafts, books, antiques, services, and all sorts of fresh and dried foods.

I cruised the isles until I found a stall with child-like charts of the human body and bottles and batches of herbs stacked everywhere. Miss Barbara Fernandez was a living legend, known and respected throughout the country for her knowledge of herbal traditions. She sat on a stool; her adequate hips poured over its sides. As I approached, she stood, all five feet of her, and reached over to grasp my hand. Her mocha skin was smooth, and her thick, wavy hair was tucked away in a big bun

"Welcome, woman, how can I be of help to you?" she asked.

"I am very sick mother, and I would like you to treat me," I murmured hopefully.

She listened intently to my story of physical woes, but seemed just as interested in gazing at my skin, my hair, my eyes, and my general aura. She took my hands in hers and held them for a moment. Her warmth and strength moved up my arms and gave me a buzz.

Reassurance filled me: *This is going to work.*

I left the market carrying a large plastic sack filled with herbs. Her last words chimed in my mind: "In two or three weeks, your energy will return, and your organs will start to be healing. It is good that you are living here. Belize will make you well."

A pewter dawn tinged with pale pinks replaced the dark of night as I walked to the dive shop, my gateway to the Caribbean Ocean. I could barely contain the excitement erupting within me as I thought of being out on the water and under the sea.

The dive boat headed toward the early morning sun. I was the only woman on board. My dive partner, Harvey, was a young, skinny guy from England who recently got certified for open water. He appeared unsure of himself and quite distracted. I tried but failed to make a connection that would serve us underwater.

There's nothing like falling backwards, head first, into the ocean from a dive boat bouncing on high seas. One minute everything — the gear, the mask, the heavy tanks — feels so unnatural; the next I'm part of the sea, bouncing in the waves, silently descending into the deep. I always felt more at home 80 feet below the surface than on terra firma. The pure oxygen high from my tank was a happy drug for my sick brain.

The ocean was dark blue; there were few fish to be seen. The floor of the sea was barren but for grasses that bent sideways as a strong current tugged at them. That current would carry us south; the dive boat would follow above and, in theory, be waiting for us when it was time to surface.

Our instructor signaled us to follow as he effortlessly floated along the sandy bottom. I looked for Harvey. He was swimming directly behind the dive master like a duckling following its mother. He had forgotten that he had a partner and should be swimming parallel to me.

I left the kid to his fears and hung back from the group. I liked it that way. Trailing behind, I felt like a happy dolphin.

Suddenly I didn't feel alone. I had the distinct impression that someone was swimming with me. I could see the group ahead and counted all seven divers. The nagging sensation prompted me to crook my neck and look over my right shoulder.

I had a new partner: a ten-foot nurse shark. Delight!

Nurse sharks are usually the most docile of creatures, and I had no sense of danger, only surprise. I had never heard of a diver being followed by a nurse shark. The shark's nose was adjacent to my flippers. If it were beside me, I could reach out and touch it. And so I slowed. It pulled up parallel to me; we swam together. Tentatively I extended my right arm outward, touching its gray, sandpaper hide with my gloved hand. It didn't react. I stroked it a few times, then removed my fingers. After all, sharks were not made to pet.

The shark was one of the coolest traveling companions I ever had. It stayed with me until I reached the group preparing to surface at the end of the dive and then vanished as stealthily as it had appeared. Wow.

As our black, neoprene-covered heads broke through the rough seas, we looked about for our ride home.

No boat? Abandoned at sea? Impossible.

A stiff breeze blew. The serene security I felt underwater evaporated; the sea tossed me around like a dog worrying a soft toy. The open ocean swallowed us in its vastness. Time passed.

The sea was beating me up—my lips chapped from the salt water; several waves slapped me hard in the face; despite my wetsuit a chill overtook my body; fatigue was tightening its dangerous grip on me. Peopled thrashed, coughed on sea water, panicked.

"There!" shouted the dive instructor.

That has to be our boat, and the driver has to be looking for us.

"I'll swim out and flag him, if you want," I shouted back suddenly filled with enough energy to save us all.

"No. No. Separation is very dangerous. Don't move. Let's use our whistles."

The whistles we carried were an excellent rescue device. A swimmer might be invisible in a rough sea, but the shrill sound of the whistle carried far across the water.

"Hey! We're here," screamed some of my little group, arms flailing overhead as the rest of us blew our noisemakers in short bursts.

At first, nothing happened.

Is the boat moving? Is it now pointing our way? Yes, yes.

The story later went that the laid-back adolescent driving the boat had motored south to what he thought was our pick-up point. He dropped the anchor, turned on his boom box, and ate some lunch. Then he took a siesta.

If there were a contest for the ugliest mutt on the island, Tootsie could have won paws down. She had the most pronounced under bite of any creature I had ever seen. This starving waif, who followed me to the beach the day of my arrival, adopted me the moment she saw me. She sat at the bottom of my stairs day and night when I was home. I now had a guard dog; if a person or another stray came near the steps, she barked. When I traveled about the island, she followed at a respectable distance, simply keeping an eye on me. I wanted to call her Ix Chel, the Mayan goddess of healing, but each time I spoke to her "Tootsie" came out of my mouth.

There is no way I am going to take this poor four-legged soul under my wing. Even if I did, when I left, she would, again, suffer and starve, I insisted to myself.

Within a week she was sleeping on my deck, eating the best dog food, taking doggy vitamins, and wearing a flea collar. I even started investigating what it would take to bring her back to the States. She was totally devoted to me, never begging, never asking for anything in return. I considered her my guardian angel as she went to the extremes of doggie loyalty to be my perfect companion.

The languorous weeks moved in tropical time as I waited for Miss Barbara's herbs, the sun and the sea to do their job. I rested, bird-watched, strolled up and down the island and spent time in the water daily. Day trips included a visit to a Mayan ruin, Altun Ha; fishing in the ocean; a boat trip to an island to see the last of the Belize manatee, those that had not been poached by the neighboring Hondurans. I island-hopped on a small, commuter plane, sitting in the co-pilot's seat, practicing in my mind the maneuvers I learned when I took flying lessons before the illness. I spent two idyllic weeks living in a shack on a Caribbean atoll.

I diligently took my herbs and followed my healing regimen for the first two months, yet my health did not improve. My disappointment was grave; I was certain that what I was doing *had* to make me healthier. Deep fatigue and symptoms related to my swollen brain and damaged organs were interspersed with lively activities. However, enthusiasm, not healthy energy, propelled me. I always ended up crashing.

I needed to look beyond Miss Barbara's cures.

The North Highway bus dropped me at a sandy dirt track that led to the sea and a village of perhaps ten shacks fronting the lapping water, inhabited by Garifuna fisherman and their families. This ethnic group was a mixture of Nigerian slaves brought to the East Indies by the Spanish in 1635 and indigenous Carib Indians of St. Vincent Island.

I sighted their shabby, board huts with thatched roofs surrounded by broken fishing nets, floats, and junk. The ubiquitous, starving dogs walked the shoreline searching for anything to eat. I could have walked into a different century but for the broken plastic I saw around every house and along the beach.

Ancient Garifuna African healing was based on the belief that loss of connection between the realm of man and the divine caused illness. Their ceremony invoked the ancestors (mine and the healers), asked for aid from the animal spirits, and utilized the four elements (water, earth, fire, and air).

Miss Isabela, a midwife and healer, lived with her family in a miniscule space. As I entered, she shooed several curious, nearly naked children outside. She wore a long, tattered dress with yellow, black and white checkers and a colored headpiece. She was full-bodied and as black as tourmaline. Kitchen wares, food, herbs, and a filthy bed where she treated people filled her tiny work area.

I told her I had come for healing; she gestured toward the bed. Candles soon brightened the dark, windowless room. She seemed to go into a trance as, I guessed, she asked our ancestors and the animal spirits about my situation, her eyes closed but moving rapidly beneath their lids.

"You have female troubles. I must do the massage treatment; your uterus is facing wrong."

Indeed, my uterus was tilted backward, but I never considered it an issue. The uterine cure was based on the belief that the womb was the woman's center, that her very being and essence were in the uterus, in the *feminine*. I considered the extreme masculine energy that imbued my life and wondered whether there was really something to that.

I lay on my back on the small, stained mattress as she seemed to reach inside my pelvis. From my vantage point, her large, muscled hands disappeared into my belly as they began a vigorous massage. She was moving my uterus back into proper position after it had sat where it was for 49 years. The pain tore at my torso; blackness hovered near. I moaned and then cried out in short bursts, digging my nails into my fists and squeezing my eyes tightly shut.

Tears seeped through. She whispered prayers as she kneaded, tugged, and pulled. My uterine ligaments would take a long time to heal. Finally, she stood, blew out the candles, and produced a paper bag of herbs which were part of her treatment.

I staggered up the road between swaying palm trees as the kids played soccer in the sand. I surely needed some R & R after that.

I made the acquaintance of a handsome Canadian named Chuck who lived down island and sailed every day. His dark tan attested to his life in the sun; his mellow countenance attested to his pot habit. I talked Chuck into a mission.

The Caye Caulker natives narrated the story of matriarch dolphins who, as old girls, would leave their pods and spend the remainder of their lives living in the environs of men. Folklore told that they made the choice to abandon their extended families to bring healing energy to people, who needed all the help they could get. I was assured that such a dolphin lived in the waters inside the reef to the north.

Prompted by only the kiss of a breeze, the sailboat floated across a sea of cyan ripples. Chuck kept a lookout with binoculars for my sacred sister. I'd read of people going to dolphin centers and spending time with tame dolphins. I craved to swim with a wild dolphin and absorb her blessed energy and wisdom. I sat on the edge of the boat, snorkel and goggles hanging around my neck like a rosary, flippers on my feet, knowing she would come. The creature that jumped straight out of the water to an incredible height was so large and so strong that at first I thought we called up a trophy marlin. I saw her out of the corner of my eye as she reached the zenith of her jump and heard her say:

"Come to me, my child. I am here for you."

It was my dolphin.

I was in the sea in less than a heartbeat and, as I dropped toward the sandy bottom, I saw her swimming to me at high speed. She spoke to me, first with a keening sound, then vivid clicking, then keening. I called back, singing through my snorkel, a humming Om sound that vibrated love directly from my heart. I had to surface for air, but immediately dove to find her waiting for me.

Is she smiling? Surely she is laughing with me.

I waved. She shook her head back. I swam toward the shallow sea floor; she followed suit. I swam up to the surface; so did she. I dove, then started twirling underwater; she followed my example! I kicked like a mermaid; she fluttered her tail. We played like this for 20, 30 minutes. Sometimes I took the lead, sometimes she did. And then, without a good-bye, she vanished.

Chuck said he had never seen anything like it.

Once again I asked myself: *Will this encounter have the miraculous effect I hope for?*

Thanksgiving passed; candy canes hung from hibiscus bushes and the smaller palm trees glittered with tinsel and Christmas ornaments. I wasn't getting well. I believed in and trusted the healers I had visited and realized that whatever was wrong with me was not responding to the native approaches, a heart-breaking revelation. Wake-up headaches with a stiff neck plagued me each morning. Sweats far worse than any hot tropical climate could produce visited me in the nights; fatigue was my constant companion. Neurological symptoms of stinging, itching, and burning throughout my body troubled me far more than the insect bites that were part of Central American living. My cognitive processing was less than stellar. So far all my efforts had failed. As much as I hated to leave my ocean paradise, the jungle called.

The H'men, the last doctor-priest of the ancient Mayan civilization, the most famous healer of Central America, resided in the mountains near the Guatemalan border. Maestro Dr. Elijio Panti was over a hundred years old and no longer practicing, but Rosita Arvigo, an American naprapathic physician, his apprentice and a true healer in her own right, had a practice near his home. I hoped to find her, this woman who had saved the ancient Maya healing traditions (and the local tropical rainforest plants needed to treat people) before they were lost to humanity.

I made a call to her clinic.

"I am very sorry, mother, but she is out of the country lecturing for some time, and her clinic is closed," said her assistant.

What was I to do? Mayan healing was my last, best hope.

I decided to go to a village called Maya Centre to try and find a Mayan healer. The village was located in East Central Belize at the entrance to Coxcomb Basin, the only jaguar preserve on the planet, established in 1986. At the time of my pilgrimage, the preserve was home to about two hundred jaguar, the largest concentration in the world. Other cats, including puma, jaguarondi, ocelot, and margay, also thrived there. A compelling need to visit the preserve drew me.

The rusted, beaten-up bus bounced away from Belize City on the Western Highway, a rutted dirt road. "The Sleeping Giant" of the Maya Mountains, a series of hills and mountains that formed a forehead, nose, and mouth and looked like a slumbering body was visible on the horizon. Eventually we turned south on our three and a half-hour journey. After leaving the population of the coast, the swamp-lined "highway" narrowed as the bus negotiated tire-size potholes, barreling along at 40 miles an hour, rattling my brain and bones. I watched for crocodiles on the sides of the road; this wilderness bush was not a place you wanted to break down.

The dry, tropical heat cooked my already fried brain. All the windows were open. A layer of red dust covered me, and I wore a bandana over my nose and mouth to help with breathing.

I thought this was supposed to be the rainy season.

The bus dropped me off during what seemed to be the luncheon and siesta hour. The small village was quiet with only chickens and pigs strolling about. A four-wheel drive track led west. A sign read: "Jaguar Preserve—5 Miles." My intuition told me someone special was waiting for me up that road, and so she was.

As I reached the edge of the village, I saw a new cement house which sported a dramatic garden—every plant that grew in Belize seemed to be flowering there. A wooden fence covered in cascading, fuchsia Bougainvillea surrounded the lawn.

"Hello," said a kind voice as a gorgeous Mayan woman, hidden behind greenery and flowers, stood up. She had classic

Mayan features, silky black hair, and black eyes that shone like polished obsidian.

"Hi," was my startled response.

"You're headed for the preserve?" she asked in flawless English.

"Well, yes, but actually I'm wondering if a Mayan healer lives in this village."

"Ah! The spirits have sent you. Please come into my home," she offered with a mysterious smile.

The inside was modern, yet decorated with many ancient Mayan influences.

"Let me get you a glass of water." The water came from a purification system, delicious and safe.

"My name is Bobbe. I'm from Colorado and..." I went on to describe my illness, the healers I had visited, my disappointment about not being able to visit Elijio Panti and Rosita, and my beliefs about the health I could find from the sea and jungle.

"And my name is Juana," she told me as she led me into a sanctuary room. "The great H'men is my relative; I am apprenticing with him. It is a very special day that the gods led you to me, and I am happy to perform a Maya healing ceremony for you."

As a choir of birds sang in the forest, silence filled the room. I sat on the floor in front of an altar as she began what I believe was a *Primicia*, an old Mayan ritual to give thanks, to worship, and to ask favors of the Nine Maya Spirits and God. My honor and gratitude for such an experience helped me drop into the sacred space she created.

"The Spirits are the caretakers of the world; Ix Chel is the goddess of healing, very special to me," she murmured with deep respect.

Vases of flowers filled the altar. Nine white flowers in bowls represented the nine Maya spirits; the number nine is sacred to the Maya. Shining crystals sat between the flowers. Juana lit many candles. She filled gourd bowls with offerings of corn. She then burned pungent, ceremonial citrine-colored copal, the frankincense of Mesoamerica, a tree resin that had been used for millennia as incense. Pieces of hard, amber-like yellow resin sat everywhere; I saw fragments of insects and flowers trapped inside. I inhaled the aromatic scent as a smoke haze softened the space, giving the sanctuary an other-worldly feeling.

Juana whispered prayers in Mayan. I heard my name several times. A sense of love, holiness, and power filled the room.

Then I had an epiphany: I saw the face of the jaguar as in a dream and knew that it was time to fully expand my cosmology to include the ultimate, mystical creature of Central America. The jaguar invoked the power and strength of the Gods and moved between the supernatural and natural worlds, the bridge between the heavens and my earthly ills. I sensed that if I could face the jaguar, I would be exposed to the greatest force in the jungle, and the encounter would heal me.

With the vision, I felt the humility needed to develop a potent faith in the unseen mysteries that the ancients believed in. "Spread the skin of the jaguar, and you spread the stars of the universe." Because they considered the jaguar a creature of the night, I would find the jaguar on its night journey and gaze into its eyes; then I would be freed.

Juana closed the ceremony with:

"Faith moves the spirits; Bobbe, have faith."

She handed me a piece of blessed copal. The copal became my treasured talisman.

A King Vulture soared high above us as Juana and I waited outside for the 2 p.m. jeep that would take me up to the Jaguar Center.

"Have you ever seen a jaguar?"

"Oh, yes. Sometimes at night the great cat will pass through my yard. Even when I don't see him from the window, I sometimes hear him."

"Do people ever see a jaguar when they visit the preserve," I asked?

"The jaguar is afraid of nothing. It is the other cats that are more elusive. The jaguar travels the trails, roads, and riverbeds. It even *sits* on the road. The wardens have seen jaguars many times as they drive in and out of the preserve. Night and dawn are very good times."

The small, open Jeep threaded its way up the double-track dirt road. A six-foot swath of grass on either side stopped at the impenetrable wall of the dense, moist forest. Coxcomb did not have a massive first-growth rainforest; it had been logged for over one hundred years. In fact, the buildings of a former logging camp now comprised the preserve center. Yet, the awe-inspiring canopy ranged in height from 40 feet to 120 feet.

A tall, hand-painted sign with a little roof protecting it stood near the visitors' center. Three old jaguar traps sat outside. I entered the wooden building and discovered with delight that it was a treasure house of information, as was Ernesto, the warden, a native of the jungle. Like Juana, he had classic Mayan features. He stood five feet tall. I paid for a bed in the dormitory building for two nights.

"It is safe for me to roam the trails alone?"

"Well," he said with some reservation, "Yes… But you should be aware of a few things. It is good to go out in the middle of the day when the big cats are resting, and it's always helpful to be in a group. Right now the only other tourists are two Canadian girls. You might try to hook up with them. Take this map if you plan to hike alone. You can also sign up for a nature walk with me tomorrow at 10 a.m. And if you are very daring, I give a jungle walk program at night — that is when the jungle comes alive. Of one thing you must be most cautious, the fer-de-lance."

"The who?"

The fer-de-lance is a highly prolific pit viper and one of the deadliest and most aggressive snakes in Belize. It accounts for more deaths than all the other snakes in Central America *combined*. It can grow to eight feet in length and, while nocturnal, can easily be stepped on during the day because it blends in well with the vegetation of the forest floor.

Horror stories abounded: An Indian bitten by the fer-de-lance bled from all the pores of his body before dying from the snake's bite. The researcher who started the preserve, Dr. Alan Rabinowitz, told of severing the head of a large fer-de-lance and then being chased by the head while the body writhed away. I was more afraid of the snake than the cats.

I found lots of juicy information on the jaguar at the center. While endangered in most of its Central American range, it was doing extremely well at the preserve. Like our thumb prints, no two jaguars had exactly the same spot pattern. The killing power of the jaguar's jaw was awesome; he was able to crunch a skull effortlessly. And the most surprising tidbit — the chances of seeing a jaguar were supposedly 17,000 to 1.

That doesn't faze me one bit.

Scratching, slithering, rattling noises filled the darkness of the small shack where I lay on a cot trying to sleep. I was alone, or, should I say, there were no other people sharing the space. A dilapidated wooden building presented no barrier for the snakes, scorpions, and tarantulas that roamed the night, hunting. Would a fer-de-lance be attracted by my body heat and slither up onto the cot? My skin crawled as I imagined a silent tarantula tiptoeing across my sleep sheet. What were all the noises? Mice? Did scorpions make noise? I clutched my penlight in my left hand, not daring to turn it on to investigate. I didn't sleep a wink.

The forest was a noisy place the next morning. Insects screeched a discordant symphony; birds answered with far more melodious song. Giant ferns, massive palms, and soaring vines filled the jungle and competed for sunlight. I was glad that I had opted for the morning tour. A trained eye and ear were paramount; Ernesto had both.

As we stopped to identity a cohune palm, a distinctive noise arose from the underbrush.

"Those are white-lipped peccary; they run in bands of up to forty animals. They love to feed on the cohune nuts. And the jaguar loves to feed on them. They can be dangerous, so let's stay out of their way."

In a deeper part of the forest, the warden halted to point out soldier ants that carried pieces of leaves far larger than their own bodies down avenues in the vegetation.

"These are leaf-cutter ants. If you look closely you will see tiny helper ants riding on their backs. Those are protector ants who defend them from flying insects, since they have their hands full, so to speak, and can't ward off enemies."

Sometime later the most putrid, overpowering smell rose from the trail.

"This is very exciting; this musky scent comes from the scat of the jaguar. They use their feces to mark their territory."

On our return to the center, Ernesto stopped at a leaning tree to point out a place where the cats sharpened their claws. The scratches were 15 inches long and four inches wide. The deep scrapes traveled up the tree.

I headed off to the river alone. The water was gently illuminated by dappled light that shone through the canopy. Monstrous trees rested on enormous buttresses. Because their roots had to be shallow to access the nutrients on the jungle floor, the trees needed the buttresses for support.

A large pool with a singing pour-over invited me into the water. I stripped and slid into the luscious, clear pond. A green, yellow, and red Toucan sat above me in the branches. Butterflies danced by. I closed my eyes, inhaled the magic, and shifted into a meditative state as the water, insects, and birds sang three-part harmony.

I could have stayed there all afternoon but the energy suddenly changed. I felt a compelling force approaching. Could it be a cat? I sighted movement high in the trees across the river.

Too high for a jaguar.

A truly scary sound began, something between a loud, aggressive roar and a bark. It vibrated throughout the forest and seemed to come from all directions at once. Terrified, the urge to grab my clothes and run naked down the trail overtook me. Then I saw them—a small band of howler monkeys. I'd invaded their territory, and they would hurl insults and steal my tranquility until I departed.

Voluminous clouds ushered in nightfall. The insect sounds rose to a crescendo. Ernesto, the two Canadians, and I met in the dark in front of the visitors' center for the "night tour." It was 9 p.m. The lights above the door revealed ugly spider webs. I looked at the girls; their body language signaled fear.

"OK, girls. So we are going out for one hour. I go first. Stay close; don't lag behind. Maybe we get lucky and see some wild pigs or a pretty little cat...or a big cat. Listen carefully because you hear many things in the jungle night."

Ernesto carried a huge flashlight. He shone the bright beam down to his feet, up the path, to the left, and to the right. Sometimes he would shine it up into the branches where a cat might be hunting or hanging out. I was surprised by the narrowness of the trail he had chosen; the jungle choked it from either side and made the going claustrophobic. The girls followed at his heels, regularly tripping him and themselves.

"Look for the cat's eyes in the branches. Maybe you can't see the cat. Maybe you just see the shining eyes."

"I'm so scared. I want to go back," said one of the ditzy girls.

"No worry. I'm watching for the snakes. The cats will not attack four people. You are safe. We have possibilities to see many wonderful animals. Maybe an armadillo."

No one had my back. The darkness behind me was like an icy hand running down my spine. But I had plans for that night and needed to learn as much as possible about moving through the jungle in the darkness. I wanted Ernesto's expertise to help me with my coming endeavor.

Whimpering sounds. That was the *other* Canadian, the one in front of me.

"I, I can't. I can't stand this. I have to go back now," she blathered.

"I want to go back too. Now," said the girl behind Ernesto.

"But we haven't seen any animals yet," I pleaded.

"We've only been out ten minutes," countered Ernesto.

"No. You take us back this instant," said the whimperer in a breathless hiss.

There was no negotiation. We turned back. Their hysteria had unnerved me. I decided to return to my quarters to center myself and prepare for what lay ahead.

Blackness. The clouds ate up the full moon and any light that tried to seep through. It was midnight, the chosen time to begin my jaguar quest. I would walk eastward toward Maya Centre and find the jaguar. I switched on my little flashlight and immediately implemented the light pattern Ernesto had used earlier that evening. The five-mile, four-wheel drive track seemed much less intimidating than the jungle path had been. I could see down the road quite a ways.

Expand my cosmology? What – am I crazy?

I swallowed my lapse in confidence and began putting one foot in front of the other. A quiet, warm breeze enveloped me as I listened to the wind in the canopy. I was sweating now, not so much from the heat as from the anticipation and the fear. Insect sounds came from within the dark jungle; the road was a quiet corridor.

The jaguar travels on the road…

Occasional, sharp noises accompanied me; the crack of a branch startled me. I could see nothing with my flashlight when I shined it into the forest, so thick was the vegetation. I moved slowly because my intention was to be there, not to get somewhere else.

Within twenty minutes, I realized that my pitiful light was failing.

Oh my God, I forgot to bring back-up batteries.

Terror wound up my body like a python encircling its prey. I felt safe with the light. Without it, the thought of being there in a night as black as pitch was nearly unbearable.

I've got to shut off the light and keep walking. That way, when I find my jaguar, I'll still have some battery power left.

I shut off the light. The night enveloped me. I stood still, heart pounding, and allowed my eyes and my senses to adapt. The dirt beneath my feet was hard, grounding me. I sensed and heard the walls on both sides of me. Feeling, if not safer, at least reoriented, I ventured onward, slower than a snail.

Movement became a new, visceral experience, like floating through an endless inkwell. Time vanished. I didn't think; I only felt.

The storm clouds parted, and suddenly the night sky provided light. It shocked me to come out of the blackness. The road ran straight ahead; the jungle walls seemed solid. I appeared to be alone, the greatest illusion of all. Just as quickly as it came, the light was taken again. I continued. But now with a shift in the winds, the clouds parted occasionally. My senses did a jig — sighted then blind, sighted then blind.

I called to the jaguar in my mind. My prayer:

Come revered tiger. Visit me from between the worlds. Bring me your power and your strength. Heal me.

After two hours, alertness melded with calmness. I was in a state of flow as the moon once again shone its light upon the road. Sitting in the very center was a huge cat. Its massive, silhouetted head faced the jungle while its body faced me.

Although I could only see its outline, it was clear that the jaguar had come — this was no lesser cat.

I stopped, not more than 30 feet away. My heart fluttered, not so much out of terror as out of awe. In my left hand I carried the piece of copal Juana had blessed and gifted me; I tightened my fingers around it. I pointed the penlight directly at the tiger and pressed the soft rubber button. He turned his head unhurriedly and looked directly at me. A measly beam of light shot outward, revealing elegant fur with black spots and huge, piercing yellow eyes, like two translucent orbs of glowing copal. I stood between the worlds and whispered my prayer again. I also prayed the cat would not eat me alive.

My flashlight died. I thanked the moon for the grace of its light. The cat was as still as a statue. And then the clouds poured across the moon. Pitch dark night. The jaguar 30 feet down the road.

What should I do? I asked myself. *I can't keep going; I could walk right into the cat. I don't want to retreat because that might cause it to stalk me.*

So I stood where I stood, charged with the energy of the encounter, and swam in reverence for the jaguar just as the ancient peoples of the jungle had. I understood their veneration.

I stood until my body ached from the immobility. An hour might have passed. The moon had not come back.

"What the hell," I said out loud and started walking straight toward where I last saw the cat.

The darkest part of the night was behind me. It was 5 a.m., and a steely dawn began to suggest itself upon the eastern horizon. Maya Centre and the civilized world were just down the road. Was my health also awaiting me at the end of that journey?

I returned home, but I would never be the same. The jaguar had come to me and given me the courage that would carry me through the remainder of my life.

It is estimated that 40% of the great barrier reef of Belize is now damaged due to global warming, ocean pollution, and tourists.

I had a second, much closer encounter with an enormous, South American black jaguar at the Belize Zoo. I stood alone at the chicken wire fence that marked off her jungle cage. She came from the shadows of the vegetation, walked to my feet, and plopped down. I also dropped to the ground and snuggled against her, feeling the beat of her heart. Her name was Ellen; she liked women. Hats off to Sharon Matola for a dedicated life creating and maintaining the zoo and doing so much for the wild animals of Belize.

Due to the dreams and persistence of Dr. Alan Rabinowitz, the Jaguar Preserve was expanded to encompass the entire Coxcomb Basin. It now receives thousands of visitors a year, including Belizean school groups.

Before I left Belize, I managed to become infested with three botfly larvae. Two died but one flourished under the skin of my scalp, eating my flesh for sustenance. It was surgically removed weeks later—

when a doctor realized what it was — a healthy inch-long maggot.

Afterword

What can I say about life after decades of such extraordinary experiences and brazen adventures? I'd like to tell you that I still heed the call I could never explain, the magnetic obsession to follow my inner urgings to explore places, people, the planet. Instead I must tell you about the way that fate wrested my life from the world of adventuring and delivered it to a very different arena of challenges.

After the initial brain inflammation and high fever that ushered in my enigmatic disease, I received disability and dropped off the face of the earth. My professional colleagues and sports-driven friends rapidly forgot I existed. What a lonely time. Thank goodness I experienced loneliness throughout my childhood and during those decades of solo travel; I had learned to live happily as a woman alone. Armed with the perseverance, determination, fearlessness, optimism, and drive I developed during my adventures, I faced the oncoming years of heart-rending physical, mental, and emotional trials.

Throughout my travels I encountered not only adventure, but also many diverse spiritual traditions. I learned how interrelated belief and living were in many cultures. I searched. Buddhism became my spiritual bedrock. Its basic teachings allowed me to experience caring and compassion for myself and others, even when I could barely think or move. I began to embody the sense of love I encountered in many places around the globe.

Metta, a daily loving-kindness practice, was my refuge even during periods when I was nearly comatose. I could lay in bed and repeat the Metta phrases in my heart: May all beings, including myself, be safe and protected; may we be peaceful and happy; may we be strong and healthy; may we love ourselves just as we are in every present moment; may we live with the deepest ease of well-being. Life changed dramatically with the disease. Yet, no matter how badly my brain and body were challenged, a well of love and joy endured.

Eight years after the illness began, struggling with severe and progressive neurological damage, I asked to be evaluated for the only malady I had not been tested for: Lyme Disease. The results were positive. The ramifications of such a late diagnosis were dire.[1] The Lyme was destroying my nervous system and ravaging my brain, my heart, my lungs, my connective tissue. I had the symptoms of rheumatoid arthritis, three heart diagnoses, a serious sleep disorder, polyneuropathy, and many other problems. Yet it was all Lyme, "The Great Imitator." Traditional medicine was (and is) horribly inadequate in the treatment of chronic Lyme. Worst yet, some doctors suggested my symptoms were all in my head and that I should seek out psychiatric counseling. My indignation toward the medical establishment rose to toxic levels.

I tried everything in those days, sensible and quacky. Nothing made a long-term difference. I attempted Lyme chemotherapy but was simply too ill to tolerate the poisonous treatment. My condition became my full-time job. Instead of searching for routes to far-off places, I struggled with visits to doctors' offices, blood tests at labs, scans at hospitals, physical

---

[1] Kim Snyder, *Under Our Skin, There's No Medicine for Someone Like You*, Zeitgeist Films (2001), an award-winning documentary about Lyme Disease.

therapy, and an arsenal of medications and supplements. My daily negotiations changed from customs officials and third world bus schedulers to receptionists, nurses, and faceless insurance companies. These activities consumed what little strength I could call up.

I had to face the fact that I had succumbed to a disease that was slowly and surely eating away at my body and my brain.

Still, miracles occurred. For no apparent reason I would start to feel better, get up and out and begin to recondition myself. I climbed as many mountains, ran as many rivers, and rode as many trails as I could with the amount of energy I could muster. Then the Lyme would get the upper hand and take me down again. I am happy that I chose to defy this devastating disease when I had the chance, defiance being another one of those wonderful characteristics that arose and took hold as I roamed the world.

Four years ago I was diagnosed with breast cancer. In an egregious case of medical negligence, my tumor was bisected during biopsy, leaving the cancer cells to spread throughout my body before my surgery. While I could manage radiation, I could not survive cancer chemotherapy because of the damage Lyme had done. I chose instead to practice an integrative lifestyle that created a physical, mental, and emotional terrain in which cancer could not thrive. Since my diagnosis, I have lived with the cancer, trying to keep it at bay one day at a time.[2] Lyme and cancer are the two most savage, daunting mountains I have climbed and also the two greatest sources of inner exploration life has offered me.

Writing these stories has taken me ten hard years. My lack of cognition and energy sabotaged the book's completion. But I have learned to put the book — and life — on hold over and over again. Each time I went under, I simply hoped that the energy to

---

[2] David Servan-Schreiber, *Anti Cancer, A New Way of Life*, Viking Penguin, N. Y. (2008)

continue would resurface and give me a chance to complete these stories about my precious existence.

Ultimately, I have come to appreciate why I traveled and adventured throughout the world — not to conquer mountains nor to prove myself, but to share the glory and solace which nature offers and to christen myself into the enormity of life. My experiences have gifted me with the awareness that I am enfolded in grace and one with all that is.

The delusion of invincibility evaporated long ago. When I stopped identifying myself as an athlete and adventuress, I discovered that I was a true warrioress and a survivor.

With all its heartaches, life has taken on profound meaning through these years of illness. While this disease is robbing me of my life, I know that it cannot take away my essence. Indeed, there are days when a sweet whiff of that essence rises, and I jump back into life for an instant of joy. You can witness such moments in the pictures on the front and back covers of this memoir. When I perish, I believe that my essence will endure and that this little book will help it to do so.

———————

...And moving forward takes feral courage,
opens the wildest
most outrageous light of all,

becomes the hardest path of all.
The firm line we drew in the sand
becomes a river we will not cross.

But the river of the soul flows on
and the soul
refuses safety until it finds the sea.

The ocean of longing,
the sea of your deeper want,
the gravity well of your own desire,

the place you would fall becomes
in falling
the place you are held...

~David Whyte, from *"Millennium"*

Acknowledgements

In deepest gratitude

To my brilliant and great-hearted friends who shared their talents and extended their encouragement and enthusiasm over the years of the writing of these stories: Chet Ananda, Wendi Dorfeld, Alex Drummond, Carol Bosserman, Herb Glover, Jill Grubb, Billy Hayes, Sally Higgins, Arlene Johannets, Joe Johannets, John Lankford, Annamaria Laverty, Jeff Lea, Kathy Lenz, John Madsen, Michele Mullins, Susan Rose, Matt Ross, Bob Rubino, Guy Tower, and David Wiggins.

To Susan Tweit and Laura Waterman, two phenomenal female authors, who inspired me and encouraged me during this long-term endeavor. And a very special debt of gratitude to BJ Wiggins, editor *extraordinaire*, for her friendship, support, and literary wisdom in reviewing the book.

To Dr. Paul Ilecki, who helped birth this project so many years ago and to my two, occasional writing coaches, Kelly Money and Robert Gatewood, for working their magic on this non-writer. When I floundered, my fellow writers at The Boulder Writing Studio were there with massive amounts of encouragement. Thank you all.

To my gifted friend, Stan Grotegut, for helping to turn my ancient photographs into living memories. To Bob Rubino of Blue Sky Photography for the awesome, fun cover shot. To Fritz Balmer of Grindelwald, Switzerland, for the gorgeous alpine silhouette photography and glacier shots.

To my Buddhist teacher, Marcia Rose, for giving me the tools to live in the moment and to heart-of-gold Robyn Erbesfield-Raboutou, my climbing coach and last/best inspiration to ascend.

Everyone who has crossed my life path has contributed in some way to this book. In gratitude, I honor each and every one of you.

To the most courageous woman I have ever known, Katherine Cameron, a fellow Lyme-challenged person and cancer survivor whose life now hangs in the balance. I know you've got my back, and I've got yours. [Kat Cameron died of metastasized breast cancer on August 28, 2012. May she rest in peace.]

And, last but not least, to my husband, Casey, who has helped to keep me going so that I could complete this book. I love you, babe.

Made in the USA
Coppell, TX
22 February 2021